≡ *The* ESSENCE *of* LIVING

☰ *The* ESSENCE *of* LIVING

Reaching Beyond Global Insanity

❖   ❖   ❖

DAVID B. BOLEN, II

NEW VERITY

PUBLISHING

Published by New Verity Publishing
726 Keene Drive
Medford, Oregon 97504
For promotional or order information only, please call:
Telephone: (503) 857-0269 or Fax: (503) 857-0274

Cover design and illustration by Sarah Cribb.
Edited by Nancy Hackleman and Patricia Bolen.
Editing assistance by Liz Enochs, Diane Johnston,
   James Pursell.
Electronic production by Rose-Merkle Design.
Printed in the United States of America by
   Commercial Printing Company Inc.

Library of Congress Catalog Card Number: 94-67371
ISBN: 0-9641909-0-7 Pbk.

ACKNOWLEDGEMENTS

This book is dedicated to those who have the courage to examine their belief systems and to explore a world of new possibilities that will help resolve personal pain and conflict. For if we are not in harmony with ourselves, then we live in conflict with the world.

I would also like to express my deepest gratitude to those people who have provided their insight, encouragement, support, and assistance in completing this project. I especially want to thank my wife, Trish, for her gift of love and for the gift of hours spent editing this book. Dreams do come true!

True greatness is when people
get over our deaths
but don't get over our lives.

Contents

PART ONE — The Transformation of Energy

PART TWO — Self-Limitation

PART THREE — Defining Your Essence

PART FOUR — Steps to Heaven

*As students of life we never
pass or fail; we just become more
aware of our possibilities.*

PREFACE

*In the invisible world of existence lies
the intelligence that eludes the scope of
our mental vision.*

Not until the technological revolution of the twentieth century has humanity been presented with more opportunities for personal learning. Through automation and computerization we have more free time and more access to information. With advanced broadcast and communications networks and extensive air travel routes, we have nearly instantaneous contact with any place in the world. Our technology allows nations, cultures, races, and religions to have greater interaction. We use human ingenuity to devise more convenient ways of coping with the basic challenges of survival. The challenges of sustenance are more simplistic because of advancements in complex technologies.

However, what we now call the civilized world represents both progress and regression. Civilization from a technological point of view does not necessarily translate into progress from a social point of view. The word "civilization" suggests improvements in technology; we assume that technology provides improved living conditions through greater convenience. But civilization has also become synonymous with materialism, the reason for our loss of identity with our true being. The great civilizations of Egypt, Greece, China, and Rome all flourished and decayed. Could we also fall victim to our technological arrogance? The transition from a primitive lifestyle to our modern world has left societies and cultures in a state of confusion. This has led to increased conflict as the world tries to adapt to a rapidly changing lifestyle.

Despite our perceived advancements, problems of health, food, and shelter still plague our existence on earth. Even with significant improvements in life-sustaining technology, we continue to behave in ways that are detrimental to our soul. After many years of wars and conflict, we are still unaware of how to avoid them. Assimilating technology without adversity is difficult to comprehend. Many generations may pass before individuals and societies adjust and adapt to the rapid changes imposed by technology. With a proliferation of scientific explanations of life and nature, old religious beliefs are challenged and sometimes discarded.

Conflict arises when old beliefs confront new philosophies and when advocates of cultural tradition try to maintain social control instead of contributing to social harmony. A price must be paid for advancement. Conflict also arises when we are not all willing to pay the price simultaneously. Some controversial issues caused by the presence of technology include abortion, pesticides, genetic engineering, pollution, overpopulation, nuclear power, military weapons, radiation exposure, and the distribution of information. Usually, when discussing these controversial topics, one person supports the use of technology because of convenience or economic gain, while another person opposes the application of technology because of the possible health and social implications. We haven't learned how to both incorporate technology and to raise our spiritual and emotional state of being. Digitizing the emotions and the spirit is not yet feasible. Without a scientific explanation, many people still defer to religion for understanding the unknown. By not realizing our inherent knowledge or true power as individuals, we become subjects to others' beliefs, social trends, and fads. Many of us unknowingly limit our awareness of nature and our state of emotional being. We subscribe to institutionalized religion, which often discourages our empowerment. Our attachment to organized religion may explain why we are unwilling to acknowledge our potential as individuals. We learn to limit ourselves by conforming to others' interpretations of reality.

Until now, the focus of education in western civilization has been to develop one-dimensional learning based on (perceived) fact regurgitation within a particular field of study. There is very little emphasis given, if any, to the relationship between intellectual knowledge and spiritual or universal knowledge. Universities teach specialized course disciplines but fail to link multiple areas of study to reflect a whole life experience. Because we don't understand all the interdependent aspects of our physical and spiritual life, the consequences of our technological advances on our environment and personal health cannot be adequately assessed.

The increased conveniences of modern living have reduced our reliance on family and community. As the world becomes closer, we are less reliant on tradition as a source of security. The mobility of modern society has left many individuals without roots and without a sense of security. This contributes to fear and an alienation of the soul. Out of our fear, we hold on to our beliefs and traditions, hoping to feel security and a sense of belonging.

Too often, our traditional beliefs only reflect our own parochial view. Through religions, political parties, ideologies, ethnic affiliation, or nationality, people worldwide are looking for security and improvements in their quality of life or standard of living. The perceived opportunity for elevating our lifestyle usually determines our association. The real question to ask ourselves is, does our platform consider the interests of others? However, instead of recognizing our similarities as humans, we continue to promote segregation by emphasizing our differences. We alienate ourselves from others by focusing on these differences and judging them as bad or wrong.

The media further serves to compound this fear and alienation. With the media's emphasis on problems, we become intimidated, believing that there is nothing we can do to avoid societal decay. However, we must expand our horizons beyond the limits of the daily newscast. Workable value systems were once handed down by close-knit communities — now the mass media, which too often avoids the inclusion of healing social values in its programming, influences many people. For example, the media has become a great promoter of sensationalized violence and destruction. Information considered "news" contains gruesome horrors. As a democratic society we do not endorse censorship, yet we allow a few media executives to decide our viewing choices. This is clearly a form of censorship. Entertainment has become a journey into the darkness of our destructive beings, and we are losing our ability to recognize the beauty of life. The continued exposure to violence keeps us controlled by fear.

A human being's generic fear of death and loneliness comes out of a need for acceptance. In an attempt to avoid rejection and isolation, we begin to act as imitators, never learning to express our uniqueness, which can make living truly fulfilling. And the media has another agenda. Fear is the key element in the success of advertising; we may not be popular, safe, healthy, attractive, successful if we don't buy the sponsor's products. We believe we can best overcome our fears by purchasing quick fixes instead of confronting the source of our fears.

Confronting our fears is a first step to recognizing our full potential. Nature has opposing dimensions — light versus dark, wet versus dry, hot versus cold. As humans, we struggle with the opposing dimensions of our ego and our inner sense. This conflict between ego and inner sense is the source of our problems in life. The ego focuses on our perceived survival needs and generates fear. Since fear is a self-fulfilling prophecy, we experience exactly what we are trying to avoid. On the other hand, inner sense focuses on allowing life to follow its inherent path of transformation. Inner sense is the essence of our being. Essence is also a self-fulfilling prophecy. When our ego surrenders and we focus on our essence, we experience the joy of living with reduced conflict. While it may not be possible to live totally without ego, we can learn that the world is a delicate structure which seeks balance with itself. We are responsible for keeping our ego in balance with our inner sense. This means confronting our fears by challenging them with the essence of what we really want to experience in life — love!

In our quest for love, we allow our ego to distract us from the essence of our desires. We become intrigued by superficial aspirations, and the world appears complex or difficult. As complex as the world may seem sometimes, it is simpler to understand when we know the essence of living. When we are less parochial in our views, life becomes less worrisome. A world focused on meeting the needs of humanity also may serve to fulfill the needs of the individual. Letting go of national boundaries and cultural biases is the sign of a world that understands we are in an age of increased interdependence. This means we must find our commonality with other people. Human diversity is a trivial topic in the grand scheme of the universe. We need a better understanding of how our decisions impact other people, the environment, and ultimately ourselves. This calls for increased empathy in our decision process, but a sympathetic or empathetic view is difficult to attain without first knowing our true feelings.

Perhaps through education and greater personal awareness we can learn how to access our emotional and spiritual resources. We are slowly learning to open our minds beyond the physical plane in which we typically operate.

The human mind can create not only technological advance-ments but also increase our spiritual awareness. This is the challenge of the future: to develop spiritual capacities that can be directed toward the benefit of humankind. By devel-oping our spirit, we can achieve a life that is in harmony with the constant state of worldwide evolution. We can empower ourselves through individual spiritualism.

An important part of individual spirituality is identi-fying the foundation of our value and belief system. Therefore, we must examine how our beliefs influence our personal behavior and contribute to personal and world conflict. Like robots, we usually act based on our social programming. Each person's values and beliefs are slightly different, based on cultural background. Family culture, which is a subset of societal culture, also affects how we perceive the world. Without understanding our thought processes or programming, it is almost impossible to live harmoniously with other humans or the environment. We either take a positive or negative view of life. Our cultural orientation contributes to our level of fear and determines our willingness to take risks to find our personal Heaven. Those who are willing to let go of tradition create space for increased individual spiritualism. This allows us to take greater responsibility for understanding our role or pur-pose on earth.

We are each responsible for enhancing the quality of our personal lives. Once we begin to see the power of our inner sense, we can begin to experience life in ways we never thought were possible. We recognize possibilities for a more fulfilled existence. We learn to be more accepting and loving, more expressive, without fear of judgment or persecution. We recognize the gifts of an abundant life. We express our individuality without fear of rejection. We become more patient, forgiving, and understanding. Most importantly, we will learn how to Live!

You need not cry, for the well is full
You need not mourn the past,
for the present is upon us
You need not grieve,
for the essence of existence is the
Transformation of form.

INTRODUCTION

*Experience happens
when you least expect it.*

I remember hearing I had to go to school to learn; it was through the learning process that I was to gain knowledge. For many years, I believed knowledge resided in schools and in formal training programs. If I did not learn according to the school's curriculum, I would not be educated and knowledgeable. Without credentials, I wouldn't be successful and people might not accept me. I learned that success leads to happiness; at least, that is what I was told. I used to believe everything I heard or read if it came from an "authority" or "expert." I never thought to question authority. No one ever described success except in the terms of money, power, and fame. As I continued through life, I was unaware that any other definition of success existed. Even while playing little league and varsity college sports, the value of winning was that it meant success. I believed success was only possible in relation to being better than someone else. I allowed external events, people, or material items to determine my self-worth. For me success was synonymous with social "acceptance."

I was unaware of any other perspectives that could lead to different possibilities and new realities. My conditioning led me to limit my thinking. I was learning that in a society, truth has limits. Unfortunately, my parents, teachers, peers, and co-workers were teaching me primarily how to be accepted in society. They, too, were limiting their thinking. This was a fine example of the blind leading the blind. In retrospect, I know it is limiting to let society define success and tell us what we should know.

The time came when I felt the need to examine life. I felt that the limits imposed by society's shallow criteria of success were too confining and unfulfilling. I wanted to find true knowledge, a true understanding of life. Despite achieving material success, I began to question my values and education. Success and happiness did not appear to be directly related. There was always another challenge to conquer, another activity to participate in, and after every victory the winner's cup was still empty. I decided I didn't need anymore empty cups. I wanted to fill the cup and taste Life!

My journey began after I ended a relationship. Though I could not define love, I thought I had found it. After the breakup, I felt totally rejected for the first time in my life. I felt out of control because I couldn't persuade her to stay in the relationship. I found myself without the person I cared for so dearly. Still, I was unaware that I was using our relationship as another way to measure my success. My attempts to win her back were unsuccessful, and I realized that healthy relationships could not be won or lost.

For the first time, I decided to take responsibility for my life. I wanted to know how I had influenced or contributed to the breakup and ultimately to my loneliness. I began to consider how I might have participated differently in the relationship. If every dark cloud has a silver lining, then this breakup was the best thing that happened to me. While examining my attitude, communications skills, and behavior, I was discovering a new perspective (a humbling experience, but enlightening). I studied other people's relationships to gain a better understanding of how people relate. My investigation was like peeling the layers of an onion. I learned about communication, anger, ego, fear, addiction, self-esteem, acceptance, peace, compromise, shame, guilt, relaxation, trust, tolerance, patience, compassion, nurturing, love, and, most importantly, myself.

During the next few years, I still believed that if I did all the "right things," I would find happiness. I used this belief in an attempt to find another love-of-my-life. I eventually realized I needed to love myself. I learned that suffering comes from our attachment to the ego, the basis of human conflict and personal drama. Our ego prevents us from trusting ourselves, from trusting others, from trusting nature. Our lack of trust prevents us from experiencing our true desires.

When I finally surrendered my ego, new opportunities began to present themselves. I started thinking in terms of emotions and spirituality instead of material and financial wealth. I thought I would feel out of control, yet I have more control. I thought I would feel vulnerable, yet I feel strong. I have taken responsibility for knowing what I want and being true to my innermost desires. I have learned to love and to nurture myself. I am learning to live in harmony with the world. I accept life for how it is and not how I expect it should be. I have overcome fears that kept me confined for many years. My view of life is now joyful. I now know that love and happiness are not things we can search for and find, but a state of mind derived from self-acceptance and humility.

In the following pages, I will share my discoveries with you. Everyone has different backgrounds and experiences that affect how they interpret their environment. The value and meaning you receive from this book will be determined by the degree of attachment you have to your beliefs and ego. Each person who reads this book will agree, disagree, find value, or dismiss the ideas based on their experiences and present state of being. Many of us are not aware that our thoughts frequently reflect our fear. We sometimes become consumed by our fears and ultimately allow fear to control our thoughts and behavior. I encourage you to explore your thoughts and evaluate the impact your fears have on your life and those around you. Eventually, you will know if your beliefs or fears are preventing you from having the life you want. You may need to create a different reality for yourself. If you feel my thoughts are too abstract or unconventional, then explore your thoughts and seek your own understanding of the essence of living. There are no answers that can be found entirely outside yourself. The purpose of this book is to expand your awareness and to encourage the use of your full capacities as a human being.

Part One gives you a chance to expand your thought process by introducing new ideas about our origin, present and future. The initial concept introduces energy as the source of our existence. It further describes the characteristics of energy, supporting Einstein's theory of relativity where energy is never lost but transformed. The transformation process begins when mass converts to energy and energy converts to mass. What I call "inner sense" determines the form that mass takes. Inner sense is the intelligence that determines the interaction of mass and energy in the universe. We are each born with inner sense, which is why we exist in the form we do. Part One of the book goes on to explain the steps we follow in the human development process. Everyone follows a similar path in life because of ego. Ego leads to dissatisfaction and ultimately to a point of crisis in our lives. From this point we either stay stuck or continue a path of personal awareness and development. We eventually rediscover our inner sense, which helps us to understand our true purpose in life. The flow chart at the beginning of Part One is an illustration of the transformation of energy as it relates to the human development process. Each phase of this process is described in Part One.

Part Two describes how we limit ourselves. This section will help you become aware of how your personality, beliefs, and fears affect the choices and decisions you make. Since you are responsible for your life, your decisions make the difference in how you feel about yourself and your life. You will read about new ways to view the things we generally take for granted, like health, relationships, work, food, attitudes, and emotions. I offer you a perspective in which to evaluate your current knowledge, beliefs, attitudes, and lifestyle.

Part Three is very exciting because it is in this section that you will discover the essence of what you want in life. Essence allows you to become reacquainted with your inner sense and discover your true purpose in life. By knowing your purpose, you will feel a greater sense of harmony. Fulfilling your purpose will bring you joy and happiness. After you use the matrix provided in this section, your purpose will come clear. You will define the essence of what you want in key areas in your life — for instance, relationships, environment, and profession. You also will learn why many of us cannot experience what we really want.

Lastly, Part Four provides some helpful hints on how to start your journey to a more fulfilled and happier life. In this section, I have summarized the general philosophy of this book. You can use this section as a reminder when you feel that you need positive reinforcement. This section discusses how you can create Heaven here on earth. I challenge the traditional belief that we must physically die and have a passing report card to enter Heaven. Instead, I suggest that you must allow your ego to die and favor your inner sense. When you let go of your ego, you will start to find the qualities of Heaven in your life. Some have described this state as magical and miraculous!

There is no substitute for individual responsibility. Please keep in mind that the ideas presented in this book are not intended to be absolute answers to overcome life's trials and tribulations. Unfortunately, many people are looking for immediate answers in life without realizing that they already know the answer. When you look internally for clues about how to create the life you want, you become your best advisor; trust yourself and listen carefully to your mind, body, conscience, and subconscious. Listening to yourself is a skill you will develop slowly. To master this skill requires honesty and dedicated quiet time. Take time to learn from the viewpoint of others; read, and listen. The information you gather will give you clues about how you might enhance your life. Instead of viewing the uncomfortable times in your life as the results of a mistake, perhaps you can see them as just opportunities for greater awareness and personal discovery.

There is no shortcut to developing your potential; there is no map; there is no final destination. There are many roads that can be chosen, but they all lead right back to you. Stay focused on enjoying the scenery as you go. The life you want can be experienced now, or later. The choice is really yours. Even as you read this book, you are on your way to creating the life you truly want!

I have written in the familiar plural (we, our) throughout most of the book because I feel we all share similar feelings and thoughts, and our emotions help to define the human life experience. The greatest emotion of these emotions is love for ourselves. When I finally realized that self-love is the most important aspect of living, I was blessed with a mate, improved family relationships, and many loving friends. I thrive in the fertile soil of loving relationships. The more I love myself the greater I appreciate my existence in this world. I share this book with you as an act of love and in keeping with my essence and purpose. I desire the same level of peace for you that I have come to enjoy as a result of the knowledge I share in *The* ESSENCE *of* LIVING.

Part One

The Transformation of Energy

❖　　❖　　❖

HUMAN DEVELOPMENT AND SPIRITUAL GROWTH CYCLE

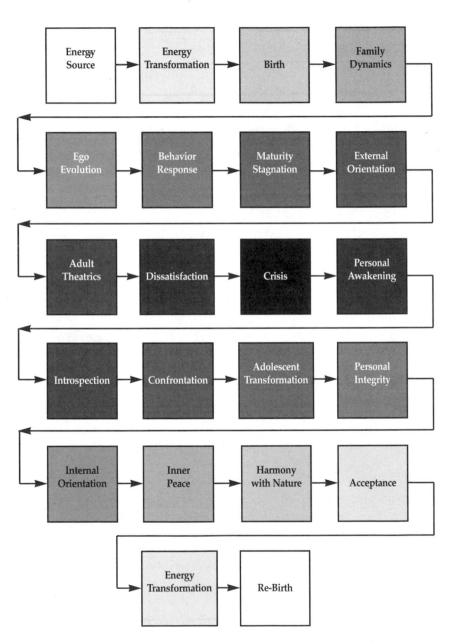

Chapter 1

The Philosophy
of Energy

We merely lease space in the universe to
accommodate the existence of our eternity
in its various forms.

Scientists, clergy, and others have been debating for cen-
turies about the origins of life. In laboratories, schools,
churches, and in homes we are still formulating opinions
and scientific explanations that describe the origins of
humans, the planet, and even the universe. We generally
think of life in terms of our own existence. The observations
we have of ourselves are usually framed in the context of
our environment and our belief system about that environment. Since we view our own lives as having a beginning
and an end, we perceive most things as having a beginning
and an end. This leads us into controversial discussions

about the origin of life.

To prove our theories of life and death, we have developed measurement techniques. If we believe in the accuracy of measurement, then there is evidence that the earth has existed for over 200 million years. However, scientific theories also suggest that humans have only existed for approximately three million years. During that time, 77 billion people have inhabited the earth. Today, approximately 5.4 billion people are participating in the human experience on this planet. This individual existence on earth appears insignificant next to these figures.

Scientists have also discovered evidence to suggest that the earth has undergone major changes in its atmosphere and topography. For example, water once covered the entire earth. By examining a globe, we notice that the continents look like they once fit together, as though the land masses connected before they separated.

What conclusions can be drawn from science and its observations? The time it takes the earth to change is almost indistinguishable from the perspective of a single human life span or even the span of several generations. As humans, we often don't recognize change in our lives as a form of transformation, but life on planet earth comes from the constant transformation of energy. Subatomic physicists have studied the origins of life by trying to split increasingly smaller subatomic particles. Quarks and antiquarks now replace the atom as the smallest known element of matter. In laboratories scientists are trying to find the beginning so that we can better understand the end, and ultimately the purpose. Cosmologists are seeking to understand how the earth fits into the larger universe. The findings of scientists looking through telescopes are surprisingly similar to scientists who use microscopes. Neither can find a beginning or an end. But scientists have discovered that the same basic particle matter is present in both cosmos, which suggests that life on earth or in space is one continuous energy field.

Science and the scope of our thoughts limit the universe as we know it because we cannot comprehend the magnitude of an entire universe beyond what we already know. We do not have the sophistication to know what exists outside our compressed universe. Our minds are really just black holes in which we exist. Our ego is the center force of gravity that constricts our thoughts.

In an exercise to expand our thoughts, let's consider that human beings are just another form of energy. If we believed we were pure energy, we might see greater possibilities for our lives. Why? Because we could see life as more than our physical form. Physical existence represents only one dimension of our existence. In addition, our thoughts and emotions are part of our existence. During the human life experience, we seldom explore the power of our thoughts and emotions, which are also a form of energy. We might, for example, by becoming aware of our thoughts and finding new ways to channel those thoughts, learn to communicate with other forms of life, both physical and nonphysical.

Opening communication with other energy allows us to see a purpose to all realms of existence. We can recognize that every form of energy has a reason to exist in its present state. We can better appreciate our purpose in life if we remove limits, increase awareness, and enhance communication with other energy forms. We can begin to understand that much of our dissatisfaction and discomfort in life is a result of our inability to feel a sense of belonging and acceptance. As humans, we believe we possess a mental capacity that exceeds other known forms of life. Unfortunately, when we see ourselves as the center and most important form of life in the universe, our arrogance becomes loneliness. By using the power of our minds (nonphysical energy), we can free ourselves from our self-inflicted isolation. When we feel connected to other forms of life, we start to feel in harmony with ourselves, and we no longer feel lonely, afraid, or alienated.

Living in harmony suggests the absence of resistance. If we are not in harmony, we are most likely in conflict. Continued conflict may cause us to experience life as limited and silently painful. Instead of creating conflict, we can complement the presence of other life. We mentally attain a state of oneness through self-awareness, understanding of nature, and compassion for all life. If we learn to respect the beauty of creation, we increase our chances to live in peaceful coexistence. We only maximize the use of our bodies and minds when we are living in harmony.

When in a state of harmony, we are most compatible with other energy in the universe. Acknowledging our unity and inevitable integration with all life allows us the freedom to experience our true inner sense. As long as we remain in harmony, we can experience a sense of belonging and acceptance with life. If we are in harmony, we recognize and accept the transformation of energy as the basis for our existence. Accepting aging and our inevitable death as part of the transformation process serves to relieve the discomforts of our human experience.

Energy Transformation

I am just a bud
I have dreamed of a season
A new world is upon me
A warm light nurtures my spirit
My fragrance smells of life.

❖

From our limited perspective we believe that man and woman are responsible for creating human life. But if we take a closer look, we realize that life is a transformation of hydrogen, oxygen, and other molecules. Without the support of a universal and intelligent chemical and electrical molecular structure, we would never come into existence. Where do these molecules come from? We don't know for sure. Some scientists support the Big Bang theory that they believe started life in the universe. Others dismiss the discussion with a nonscientific approach that credits God with the formation of the universe. The least obvious alternative to us as humans is the theory of perpetual transformation, which suggests there is no beginning and no end. Since there is no conclusive evidence, we cannot trace the origins of the universe at this point in history. What we do know is that molecular particles are energy and transform from a previous place and time. In 1905 Einstein discovered the theory of relativity. His theory tells us that E (energy) = m (mass), and the transformation can be measured by multiplying mass times the square of the speed of light. Einstein suggested that atomic particles are mass and therefore energy. He further believed that mass is simply energy in a resting state that loses energy to another mass as it transforms. We can suppose that the rate of transformation relates to the amount of energy an object has. So, for example, during the transformation process, energy as mass converts to motion or heat. In restating Einstein's theory we can also say that Energy = Transformation = Existence. This idea is hard for many of us to grasp because we have learned to think in terms of tangible experiences.

If energy can present itself in any form it chooses, then everything that exists is energy. Therefore, I have chosen to refer to mass that cannot be seen by the naked eye as nonphysical energy. Even things that are not visible or tangible to our five senses (touch, sight, smell, hearing, taste) are energy.

Energy in all its forms is interdependent and responsible for the human experience. Energy provides our atmosphere, the plants we eat, the water we drink, the sounds we hear, the thoughts we think, the feelings we experience, and the things we create. Our reality shapes the interaction of our thoughts and nervous system with these other forms of energy. All things, seen or invisible, real or perceived, consist of energy in the physical or nonphysical realm. Energy exists in the pages of this book, in the chair you are now sitting on, in the light bulb, in light waves, in electricity to power the light bulb, and so on. If it were no longer possible for any of these items to exist, it also would mean that we would cease to exist.

A certain and exact set of conditions must exist in order for energy to transform or remain in a resting state. Everything in the universe would stand still in a state of suspended animation if energy actually stopped. Instead, energy converts mass to a particular molecular structure temporarily. For example, it only rains, snows, or mists under a certain set of conditions. Energy can transform from snow to water and even to a vapor if the circumstances so dictate. Likewise, humans can only be born under an ideal set of conditions, and energy transforms molecules into a structure that we know as the human experience. Various forms of energy must combine in the correct formula and under the ideal conditions to create human life. As far as we know, this set of conditions only exists on this planet. Consider mixing chemicals in a test tube; given the correct formula, an explosion or perfume can result. The outcome is a result of the transformation process. The human experiment also can be viewed as self-destructive or constructive — and even enlightening.

Human life, like everything else in the universe, is in a temporary state of existence. Since our physical being is not a permanent form of energy, we will transform to another state of existence. Our bodies are like large batteries. We can recharge our bodies through nutritious food, exercise, and rest. The cells in the body store the energy that is integral to our health and survival. Energy powers our brain, immune system, nervous system, digestive system, and cardiovascular system. There are many other examples of energy in nontangible forms that affect our lives: gravity, light, sound, heat, wind, thoughts, to name a few. Each of these forms of nontangible energy can be transformed when interacting with physical energy. For example, the wind can put a propeller in motion that in turn can create electricity that in turn can create light, and so on. So why do we fear the inevitable transformation of our being when our energy never dies? Why do we attach so much meaning to life in our human form? The answer may lie in understanding the development of our ego and the diminishing awareness of our inner sense from the time we are born.

Life is just an experiment.
We live in a test tube,
where we are constantly mixed and tested
to see how we will react or respond.

Chapter 2

The Human Experience

Birth

A homeless note searches for a flute
The flute said, "I am empty without the wind
Send the breath of life through my body"
A spirit started to blow and
The note awoke the silence
And life heard a rejoicing melody.

At birth the human mind, body, soul, and spirit are truly one; we call it innocence. Ironically, it appears that innocence comes from the word " inner" and the word "sense." We are energy born with inner sense, the intelligent energy that forms our molecular structure; it is the essence of our existence. At birth we still experience a sense of oneness with nature, similar to having been in our mother's womb. Unfortunately, the more we interact with the world outside the womb, the more we lose an awareness of our inner sense because we begin to realize our separateness from all that surrounds us.

Can you remember what you felt when your umbilical cord, your lifeline, was cut? How many of us remember how we felt when we went from a constant temperature, wet environment to the world outside the womb? We don't remember because we went from a state of inner peace to a world of confusion where we were no longer one with the environment that created us. At birth we lose the security that the womb automatically provides for us. We develop a sense of self (ego) and we learn to ask for what we need. We use crying as our first form of communication. Our inner sense remains active until we become less dependent on our mothers. Meanwhile our ego continues to evolve as we explore our independence.

Ego is precisely what fascinates us about human conception, birthing, and maturing. We see human life as a miracle because our ego insists that we are more special than anything else in the universe. If we would learn to appreciate the transformation of energy, we would recognize that human creation is neither more nor less miraculous than the universe itself. We are merely an integral component of an interdependent world of energy. When energy transforms itself into human life, it provides us with the necessary intellectual and physical attributes to survive. We inherently know how to interact with other energy forms to ensure our survival for some indefinite period. Through the aging process and death, inner sense has the intelligence to transform us. By becoming acquainted with our inner sense and understanding the essence of living, we can experience the comfort of the oneness that we felt in our mother's womb.

Our challenge in life is to rediscover our inner sense. Unfortunately, after we are born we must experience maturing and growth, starting with our introduction to the family.

Family Dynamics

The condition of unconditional love is love.

A family consists of others who nurture and interact with us (as newly transformed energy) to help preserve our existence. The family interacts with us primarily in the physical realm and in the nonphysical realm by transferring emotional energy such as anger, fear, or happiness to us. How the family responds to our needs affects the development of our psychology and personality at a very early age. For instance, during infancy we establish behavior within the family. We learn how our basic survival needs will or will not be met. Because energy is in a constant state of change, our interaction with the family is dynamic and therefore inconsistent.

As children, we are oblivious because we are sometimes pawns in the emotional warfare that exists between parents. We are sometimes unknowingly manipulated to take sides as one parent tries to gain an advantage by using us or our siblings to balance the relationship. Unfortunately, it is the family environment that, while responding to our survival needs, also shames us through manipulation, scolding, spanking, beating, verbal abuse, silence, molestation, and other forms of defeating parental rituals. Previous generations learn this kind of behavior and pass it along through our parents. Abuse may also occur when our parents react to stress caused by their fear; they pass along their fear by threatening us with words like, "You'd better...or else...", or

"If you don't...I'm going to...". In response to these destructive tendencies, we seek to regain our sense of safety and value inside the family. We learn to play a role that we believe best limits or overcomes the abuse. Additionally, we seek validation outside the family by developing relationships that either reinforce our family experiences or give us a chance to develop a healthier pattern of behavior. In either case, we strive to be accepted, and our ego motivates us to fulfill our need to be validated. Thus, the ego is the first element of our personality to evolve.

As we grow up with family members, who are also ego-based, our fears become substantiated. Much of our perception about how safe and secure our world is originates from the dynamics of the family environment. During infancy we receive information from our families that tells us how much to trust other people. As ego and fear begin to create our perception of reality, we develop personality and behavior traits designed to protect ourselves. Those traits become our script for the role we play in life, the only reality and possibility that we trust. For example, neglect may lead to a fear of abandonment. This may cause us to overcompensate for the perceived rejection from the family, and we seek attention and acceptance.

On the other hand, overprotecting parents may cause us to suffer from an overdeveloped ego (an overdeveloped ego refers to the imbalance between one's ego and one's inner sense). In this case, we may need constant reinforcement to maintain a perceived level of security and acceptance. If we are overprotected as children, we need to be reassured of our importance, and we may become emotionally dependent and fragile.

The balance between overprotection and underprotection is difficult to achieve if fear and ego consume our caretakers. For example, our parents' dispositions and the quality of their marital relationship influence how we develop emotionally. Also, confusion can arise when we listen to mixed messages coming from multiple caretakers in an extended family model, which includes relatives, stepparents, day-care, school, nanny, or babysitter. (For many families, the television is also a part of the extended family.) Since ego plays an important part in our personality, we need to be more aware of the influence ego has in our lives and in the lives of those around us (especially our children). Our children can learn to live from their inner sense if we as parents set the example. Otherwise we are inflicting our insecurities and fears on our children, ultimately limiting their potential.

Ego Evolution

The hand that holds the child
touches the future.

A misunderstood aspect of human existence is that of the ego. What is ego, anyway? The term ego, in this book, refers to the mental energy that creates the illusion of separateness. Historically, ego is a term that defines the distinction of the self or the individual. So we generally associate selfishness with ego. As we grow, we become further aware of our separateness from our mother and other forms of life. In an attempt to protect our ego or self, we establish behavior that ultimately forms our personality. Some of us believe ego is good because it is essential to our survival. I believe that too much ego can be detrimental to our socialization and can cause us to become selfish, losing our compassion for others. When we are selfish, our primary interest is seeking gratification or survival.

As we grow up and become more aware of our independence, we realize that we are responsible for our own physical and emotional survival. From birth, fear engulfs us with thoughts of not having our basic survival needs met. We lose confidence in nature to provide for us. Our ego is, therefore, fear based. We become externally focused, always looking out for threats to our physical and emotional well-being. Even during adulthood we perceive that our existence is in jeopardy. What we fail to realize is that while we have responsibility for our lives, our survival depends on how we interact with other forms of energy. Therefore, placing our own importance over that of other energy forms denies our interdependence for our existence with other forms of energy. There is no such thing as separate and more important energy in an interdependent universe. Everything that exists has purpose in perpetuating the transformation process. As long as we believe we are separate from everything else, we will experience a lonely existence filled with conflict. Unfortunately, most of us maintain the belief that we are truly separate from other forms of life.

To better understand separateness, let's examine how ego evolves and creates our reality. The brain is electrical and chemical energy. It acts as our resident pharmacist and dispenses chemicals to our bodies. Internal or external stimulation alters the chemical balance. Internal stimulation (emotion) is inherent to the human species. External stimulation (physical pain and pleasure) comes from the interaction with energy that affects our physical being. External events influence our physical and mental state of being and trigger our thoughts that solicit an emotional response. Thoughts, derived from our ego, or fear, lead us to become oriented toward external events (external orientation). We become watchful of things that might threaten us. Instead of being introspective and realizing our potential for harmony with all energy (internal orientation), we stay trapped by our fears. Ego focuses our attention externally to help us avoid potential threats to our survival or happiness.

Since ego is the alarm that alerts us to potential danger, it prepares us for conflict and protects us from anything that threatens our survival. Therefore, we believe that ego is a positive and necessary element of our personality. However, since ego correlates with fear, it stifles the development of our other emotions. For example, when fear consumes us we become highly focused on protecting ourselves instead of experiencing other emotions, like trust and love, that allow us to live a more fulfilled life. Ego and fear cause us to be reactive in life as we try to avoid perceived threats. Unfortunately, we do not always know when we are acting out of fear (or from our ego). Most people who fear abandonment, rejection, pain, or death are externally oriented. The ego- or fear-based person worries more about what other people are thinking than about experiencing their feelings and true desires. This state of overexternalization leads us to dissociate from others and from our inner sense. Thus we prevent ourselves from being in harmony with nature and experiencing inner peace.

When ego and fear are the predominant aspects of our personality, they create stress. Too much stress creates a chemical imbalance in our bodies and ultimately leads to ill health. We are, in varying degrees, either healthy or sick, happy or sad, depending on how fearful or ego-invested we are. Emotions and physical sensations determine how we experience life. Good health closely relates to how we maintain harmony with our inner sense. We need to develop trusting relationships with ourselves and other forms of energy if we are to experience inner peace. If we consider that, as energy, we never cease to exist, then we also might realize that it is our inner sense, and not our ego, that is responsible for how long we live in our physical bodies. We would realize that we never die, we just transform to another state of existence. With this knowledge we can accept our inevitable transformation as one of life's experiences; we can live happier lives. In addition, we can let go of our ego, regain an awareness of our inner sense, minimize conflict, and create harmony with other humans, nature, and, most importantly, ourselves.

Ego, which reinforces our separateness, is the opposite

of inner sense. We create our own perception about life based on the fear that our ego generates. Inner sense gives us an awareness of our connection and allows us to be in peaceful coexistence with all other forms of energy. Ego protects our separateness, and inner sense protects our unity with other energy. Ego suppresses our intuitive abilities or inherent awareness of knowledge. Inner sense, by contrast, causes us to be proactive by allowing our intuition instead of our fears to guide us. Inner sense gives us the opportunity to reduce conflict and live a more satisfying life. To us, of course, perception is the same as reality. Therefore, if we do not balance our ego with inner sense, we lose our ability to distinguish possible realities from limiting perceptions. The following chart shows the characteristics that we possess when we live from our ego instead of from our inner sense.

ENERGY TRANSFORMATION

EGO vs.	INNER SENSE
FEAR =	**ESSENCE =**
REACTIVE	PROACTIVE
LOGICAL	INTUITION
RULE BASED	CREATIVE
LIMITS	POSSIBILITIES
JUDGMENTAL	OPEN-MINDED
VICTIM	FREEDOM
WORRY	TRUST
ILLNESS	HEALING
CONFLICT	PEACE
SEPARATENESS	HARMONY

Behavior Response

*We are all products of conditioned behavior
induced by years of knowing only
our own environment.*

Now that we understand our ego, we can better appreciate how our physical, emotional, and intellectual development affects our behavior and vice versa. As stated, certain behaviors evolve from an environment where a conditioned response ensures our survival. As we grow up, our families usually change their expectations about what behavior is appropriate for us. For example, our parents may choose to let us cry instead of rushing to see if we are all right; they may postpone feeding or avoid consoling us. Neglect feels threatening and leads to panic. We become concerned that our needs will not be met. When old behavior doesn't produce the anticipated results, it creates conflict because we want to hold on to our established childhood behavior. We maintain our behavior because we have different perceptions of what is necessary for our well-being or socialization. Ultimately, in our confusion we experience fear.

An example of how behavior evolves can be observed with those who experience drowning. Panic sets in and the drowning persons' behavior becomes more pronounced as they struggle to survive. Of course, the family on the sideline yells to them to remain calm. Panic keeps those drowning from hearing or listening because their fear is all consuming. Once they perceive that they are safe, they will calm down. However, their memory banks record the fearful experience. In an attempt to avoid repeating the situation, these persons will modify their behavior. In these frightening experiences, we also record how our caretakers respond. We learn what to expect from our families.

As we explore our independence from the family, we gain a greater awareness of our ability to take care of our personal needs. These experiences become programmed in our minds as either positive or negative. Negative programming affects our level of self-confidence and determines how we handle future situations. New situations trigger our memory and we demonstrate aggressive or passive behavior, honest or dishonest behavior, or we act securely or insecurely, based on our experiences.

During our development we begin to test behavior boundaries. The results or reactions to our behavior influence our personality evolution and we choose what works best for us. We then take on roles, such as perfectionist, comedian, troublemaker, introvert, extrovert, martyr, and so on to get our needs met.

So as children we become ingrained with the belief that certain behavior solicits a desired response. This behavior may be acceptable within the family environment but may be unacceptable outside the family. Temper tantrums or pouting are examples of behavior that may not transfer well outside the family. Reaction from outside the family further reinforces or disproves our beliefs about behavior. When we enter school and succumb to peer pressure, we can observe this situation. As we test the boundaries of our behavior, we often modify our behavior and manipulate our environment to have our physical and emotional needs met. For instance, the need to be accepted and validated is often why we try to excel in music, sports, academics, art, or other endeavors. Another way we seek attention or acceptance is by resorting to aggressive or destructive behavior. Some of us start lying out of fear that we will be rejected or will experience physical or emotional pain if we tell the truth. Even during adulthood it is not uncommon for us to lie to "save face" and maintain our position on the job or in a relationship. Unfortunately, while focusing on behaviors that we feel ensure our acceptance, we deprive ourselves of the natural maturing process that allows us to feel comfortable with who we really are (inner sense).

Maturity Stagnation

Wind does not blow
in the leaves of a winter's tree
nor in the sails of a sunken ship.

Maturation is the growth process that allows us to relate to life with an open mind. However, as we identify behavior that consistently produces the desired result, we lock into that behavior and cease to mature. Unless we test new boundaries and patterns of thought and behavior related to our survival, we will cling to our "tried and true" behavior out of fear. This means we shut down to the possibilities that we can experience life differently, and, instead, we choose to relate to life from the perspective of our defined childhood role.

Even though the experiences we have during infancy mold our personality and disposition, typically there is an incident or a series of traumatic incidents that occur during childhood or early adolescence (usually between the ages of seven and seventeen) that cause us to enter a state of shock. The traumatic experience could be a death in the family, divorce, physical abuse, rejection by a girlfriend or boyfriend, failure to meet expectations, or an embarrassing situation. These experiences hinder our emotional maturation; it is as if we become frozen in time. We lose the confidence and the trust we have in ourselves and others. We become consumed with fear that we will experience further pain. Most people in adult bodies are still living at a younger level of maturity, despite how they may appear outwardly to others. Many adults develop disguises to give the impression they are strong, assertive, successful, or influential, while they are instead really feeling scared and insecure. Others become martyrs and convince themselves they are not capable of or entitled to a more abundant life. This occurs because they have never resolved the traumatic incident in their life that led them to the conclusion that they will be rejected, abandoned, or devalued.

There are many ways that we choose to cope with our trauma. Unfortunately, most of us seek relief from the exact thing that caused us the pain. For instance, if we feel rejected by a parent or boss because of our behavior, we may become obsessed in our attempts to have that person accept us. Our ego wants us to be liked. We try to avoid the pain of rejection by using our tried and true behavior or personality (which is how we alienated the other person to start with). If our initial attempts to be accepted don't work, we may dissociate from our pain by turning to alcohol, drugs, or living in the past, waiting for things to be the way they used to be. Rejection causes us to panic like the drowning swimmer. We seldom see the possibility that we can experience the essence of our desires by focusing introspectively. Our watchful eye, instead, stays alert, looking externally for future threats and blaming other people for our rejection. We tend to stay attached to the physical form of our memories and thus expect the future to be like the past. We resist changing our viewpoint because we want to feel in control and safe, and we don't trust that our inner sense will provide for us. The ego maintains control and we stay externally oriented and stuck in the drama of our lives.

External Orientation

You are not where you think you were,
which is why you can't get there from here.

Because we think we know what we want, we spend our lives looking for material or physical satisfaction, hoping for happiness. But contrary to popular belief, fulfilling desires of the ego will not inherently bring lasting happiness. What we don't do is consider altering our beliefs, behavior, or attitudes. Once we are old enough to spend time away from the family, our motivation is to determine, ensure, maintain, or enhance our level of acceptance and significance. Therefore, we seek out ways to feel validated by trying to gain acceptance from a nonfamily social structure. Once we enter school, we find security in a pseudo-family known as a clique. While in school, most of us worry about being likable. We use dress, hairstyle, musical taste, speech patterns, language, and other themes as criteria for acceptance.

To ensure our acceptance, we first test the behavioral role we play in the family. If this is unsuccessful, we begin to modify our behavior in an attempt to solicit the response we feel is necessary for our acceptance. Again, we change who we are to adapt to external influences, and this leads us another step away from our inner sense. We surprise our naive parents when they find out we behave differently away from the family. Many parents who are unaware of their child's emotional state defend their child with the classic statement, "Not my kid! He/she would never do anything like that." Unfortunately, we learn, "When in Rome do as the Romans do." It's not surprising that we give up our individualism for social acceptance. Our parents want us to be liked or popular because it helps to satisfy their egos to say, "Our kid is smart, first, the best!" We seldom learn that we are acceptable without having to prove it.

In an attempt to find gratification and an end to our life drama, we think we can relieve emotional pain by avoiding the things we don't want. This is a fear-based approach to life because it is reactionary. Unfortunately, this external orientation, which drives most people, becomes the basis for our pseudo-adult behavior. In other words, in terms of our behavior maturation as children, we never make it past adolescence. We get stuck with the ingrained recordings of family behavioral dynamics and values imposed by the social groups with whom we associate.

Adult Theatrics

*There is no greater drama
than that of an unconscious being.*

From the teenage years, our emotions seldom make the transition to adulthood. We continue to allow ego to control our emotions while we neglect our inner sense. As adults, most of us are still operating from an adolescent state of mind. Because our inner sense is dormant, the ego dominates by providing a script that we act out. What this means is that many of us are imitating what we believe is an "adult" lifestyle; we smoke, drink, get married, have children, buy material goods, and try to climb to professional success.

One day I was at the checkout stand of a department store, and I noticed a stack of large boxes containing a child's toy kitchen. On the front of the box was a full-color picture of a boy and a girl about age five. The girl was talking on a play telephone and the boy was watching with delight as they stood in this play kitchen. It occurred to me that the manufacturer is marketing this toy to parents who want their children to be adults as soon as possible; we learn at a young age how to "act like an adult."

When we become teenagers, exploration of our independence from the family is typically of paramount interest. At adolescence, we begin to feel the confidence to make independent decisions. We believe we are adults. During adolescence our ego becomes fully mature. Most people think that teenagers are freewheeling and following their inner sense. This is usually not true. Teenagers are as much confined by social rules as are adults. Our ego usually develops its own version of "common sense," the rational, logical side of a person who conforms to the laws of society to satisfy the desires of the ego. Teenagers use common sense to ensure their acceptance in their clique of choice.

But our lifestyle is a response to the ego and the programming that tells us what we "should" do. The search for a healthier or more affluent lifestyle is the reason we consume so much energy trying to change our lives in the elusive search for gratification. Sometimes our superficial desires lead to obsessions and are a source of dissatisfaction and suffering. During the Adult Theatrics phase of development, a person becomes externally oriented and motivated. Artificial stimulants, drugs, sugar, sex, alcohol, money, and food, are examples of ways we attempt to add happiness to our lives, often with adverse affects. By striving for happiness externally, we block the knowledge of our purpose in life and we fall out of harmony with ourselves and nature. We become stressed and suffer from high blood pressure, heart attacks, cancer, muscular sclerosis, and other diseases. Our ego remains intact until we become introspective, usually much later in life. If we remove the masks that we wear to satisfy the ego, we can start to rediscover our inner sense.

Dissatisfaction/Dissociation

You cannot change your life.
Your life will change you.

Chasing happiness by trying to satisfy the ego ultimately leads to unhappiness and disappointment. In an
attempt to alleviate dissatisfaction, we seek to reinforce and
satisfy the ego with increasingly superficial desires. A
vicious cycle develops that leads to greater levels of unhappiness. We seek relief from the suffering through addictive
or compulsive-obsessive behavior designed to allow us, the
victims, to dissociate from our pain. The addiction can
manifest itself in many forms. An addiction implies that a
person focuses too much on a particular aspect of life. An
addicted or compulsive person becomes obsessed with an
activity to the point of ritualistic behavior. The artificial
stimulants or material items used to satisfy our ego do not
bring us closer to the essence of our true desire. The desires
of the ego lead us to actions that are inconsistent with our
inner sense. When our ego is not in harmony with our
inner sense, we experience physical and emotional discord.
This conflict eventually results in a level of dissatisfaction.

The lack of balance between ego and inner sense sets us
up for a fall. Not until inflicted with enough pain will we
admit our lives are out of control. Those of us with a strong
attachment to our social identity may stay in a state of crisis, denying that anything is amiss. Eventually we hit the
ground, and the impact of the fall transforms our energy
either physically, emotionally, or both. In other words, we
eventually suffer from poor mental or physical health.
Unfortunately, most people perceive the way out of this
cycle is to use their intellect or logic. Logic relates to the ego
and therefore keeps us trapped as we continue to try to

"fix" our problems. Inner sense, though, is intuitive and sometimes defies logic. Learning to listen to our inner sense is the way to recovery and happiness. When we follow our inner sense, we realize there is nothing to fix. Problems become merely circumstances that exist to transform our energy into a state of harmony. These troubling experiences can also be opportunities for personal learning and healing.

Crisis

An intersection
is the convergence of opposites
heading in the same direction.

Self-destructive behavior and an inability to cope with life's experiences define a point of crisis in our lives. We are in crisis when our personal suffering leads to the destruction of the ego. We become aware of our crisis when we feel our lives are out of control. While being out of control is not a bad thing, the ego-based person perceives it as disastrous. Realizing that our world is collapsing can be devastating; it can feel like a chain reaction of catastrophic events. Some of us even have a propensity to be accident-prone, or we may experience a divorce, illness, loss of a job, or financial difficulties.

We know we have reached a point of crisis when we consider changing our values or behavior. Since many of us view our lives from the perspective of the ego, it is only through this frame of mind that we recognize problems. However, when ego determines that our reality is problematic, our physical and mental health enter a state of decay. Remember, ego causes fear, and fear is a self-fulfilling prophecy. Any time we get sick we are experiencing a decay of the ego. Illness is a clear signal that we are out of harmony and not living from our inner sense. Crisis is not necessarily confined to our physical health. We may be in excellent physical shape but may experience emotional pain or depression. It is an attempt by our inner sense to inform us that we are out of balance. When we suppress our inner sense, we do not live in harmony with nature or ourselves.

When we are in severe pain, our ego surrenders and we forget our fears. We may decide that we do not wish to repeat the behavior that led us to crisis. In extreme cases, we will even commit suicide. Essentially, we know we need to make changes in our lives, but we may not know where to start. A crisis leads us to explore possibilities that may improve our circumstances. Provided the crisis is not disabling, some people will simply choose to make lifestyle changes, for example, reduction of alcohol intake, increased exercise, or dieting. While these are positive steps to improve one's life, these activities require "doing" something to fix ourselves.

Society conditions us to believe that we must "do" things. We learn to believe that it is what we do in our lives that creates our state of "being." This is a common misconception. In fact, the things we "do" acting out our adult theatrics is what leads us to crisis. It is very common to find that activities designed to resolve the crisis only offer temporary relief, and within a short period we are in trouble again. The reason? Our focus is too much on "doing" things differently. If our actions fail to show immediate results, we judge ourselves and feel guilty. Then we are back in the cycle of trying to do something else to make ourselves feel better. We generally don't have the patience to watch the transformation or to allow our lives to provide what we deserve and want.

The key point here is that we must stop trying to "do"

something to resolve the crisis. The exit to the crisis is through our state of "being." In other words, we must "be" different to initiate a state of recovery and maintain health. Again, our state of "being" determines the things we do. It is very important that a person in crisis starts by admitting and recognizing that the crisis exists. We must also admit that we are personally responsible for the crisis. This means we acknowledge how we contributed to our own pain, not blaming someone or something else. If we cannot see how we contributed to our crisis, we will return to a state of adult theatrics, dissatisfaction, and yet another crisis.

The road to recovery is to dissociate from the ego and become reacquainted with our inner sense. People who live according to their inner sense will not perceive an event as a crisis but as a reminder to live true to their essence. Inner sense gives us a true sense of security and comfort, and we don't feel threatened.

Chapter 3

☰ Personal
Evolution

Personal Awakening

The treasure hunt ends when
the pirate finds his buried spirit.

To avoid further crisis and to make our lives more rewarding, we must begin to enter a state of personal awakening. This allows us to understand where we are with respect to our inner sense. We may discover that who we really are (inner sense) is different from what we do or who we think we are (ego). By understanding this distinction, we can let go of things in our lives that are not in harmony with our true selves. We may develop a growing awareness about how we arrived at a point of crisis. Personal awareness means recognizing how our beliefs, personalities, attitudes, and behaviors cause others and ourselves to feel discomfort or pain. This insight helps us to accept the past and helps us to realize that possibilities for a more gratifying future exist. Through personal awareness, we begin to accept responsibility for our past and present behavior. To maintain a state of inner peace, we must stay inwardly focused. This is particularly challenging in a world which pivots around the demands of the ego. The external world acts as a vacuum that draws constantly at the ego, which tries to suck us back to a false sense of reality. We must stay personally alert to avoid becoming victims of ego pressure and fear.

Being aware does not keep us from acting in ways that create disharmony in our lives. However, if we are aware, we can learn to modify our thoughts before we act in ways that are hurtful to ourselves or others. In other words, we can use our personal awareness to avoid old, undesirable behavior. We can make sure that our actions are consistent with the essence of what we want in our lives. We can move away from superficial relationships and find friendships that encourage personal discovery. We can begin to surround ourselves with people who are also seeking a more spiritual life experience.

Introspection

Appreciation of life begins
by nurturing yourself.

Many of us are where we are out of circumstance and not by our choosing. We need to ask ourselves: What do I really want in life? How will I get there? Will I be happy?

Why will I be happy? Introspection is a time of contemplation and self-evaluation, a significant step toward becoming reacquainted with our inner sense. Introspection allows us to understand what lifestyle is really most fitting for us.

During the period of introspection we may feel our jobs are less satisfying, especially if we are working primarily for the paycheck. The work environment typically forces us to be externally oriented. The workplace is where we worry about what other people think of us. Our bosses evaluate us on how we act and the things we do — not on who we are. Typically, we receive no recognition for the value of our "being." We can balance this lack of acknowledgement by developing life enhancing extracurricular activities.

Even when we are unemployed we can enhance our quality of life and lifestyle by examining our lifestyle choices. We can schedule our free time to seek knowledge about how we relate, communicate, and interact with people and other living things we bring into our lives. Depending on how motivated or open-minded we are, the process of learning about ourselves may take years. Remember, as we uncover our essence, we are guided in the direction of our purpose. We must learn to be patient during this period and avoid any sudden changes that might be motivated by an uncomfortable circumstance. It is important that we don't run away from our pain, but instead become aware of what we want. Otherwise, we are very likely to recreate similar uncomfortable circumstances. We can eventually recognize how to use our past and current situations to help guide us to the essence of our being. We must ultimately identify a direction and purpose for our lives in order to reach a state of inner peace.

Confrontation

Discovery is knowing
what you didn't think you knew.

When we are ready to confront issues in our lives, we enter the growth and expansion phase of our personal development. This is when we commit to resolve conflict in our lives. Also during this period, progress feels like we take two steps forward and one step back. This means we sometimes act based on old behavior. While this is a humbling process, it is important to recognize how much of our past we carry forward. During this phase, our personal awareness keeps a check on our subconscious mind to make sure we do not sabotage our good intentions. We then can operate from a very conscious and deliberate level of thought. Though ego clouds our inner sense, we begin to allow our ego and inner sense to coexist. We immediately want to confront issues that are preventing us from having the life we want. We attend workshops, therapy, go to seminars, and read books that were previously off limits because our pride dictated that we were fine just as we were.

While it is exciting to feel we are making progress, we must be careful not to become addicted to the personal growth process. While professing to be on a path of self-development, many of us fail to live from our souls. We don't gain the benefit of our awareness because we are masters at intellectualizing our problems and the solutions. We are less proficient at implementing lifestyle changes. Real progress is possible when our focus stays on creating the life we want every minute of every day, not because it is trendy or socially advantageous, but because it is essential if we are to fulfill our purpose.

This is a very rewarding and empowering time in life.

We experiment with our intuition and don't worry whether or not the decisions we make are from our inner sense. We learn to trust this inner sense. Trusting our intuition for the first time may feel like we are jumping off a cliff into the darkness; we need a major leap of faith. As the inner sense gains prominence, we recognize a more fulfilling life. If our actions are not consistent with the lifestyle we want, we need not get discouraged. We don't have to feel guilty about the hot fudge sundae, the cigarette, or the drink we just had. While in a state of personal transformation, we sometimes act from our ego and sometimes from our inner sense. Eventually, our inner sense plays a greater role in the decisions we make. Our inner sense will be the predominant part of our conscious thoughts, just like our ego used to be. When we follow our essence and learn to act from our inner sense, we graduate to adulthood.

Adolescent Transformation

You will soon find where you are is
where you always were before you woke up.

Most people have a difficult time making the transition from adolescence to adulthood. Many people stay stuck in their adolescence until they die. They live their whole life in adult theatrics, in a world driven by their ego. They cannot understand why they don't have everlasting happiness. Happiness eludes those who try to satisfy their ego. There is always something missing, something else to conquer, another game to win. In the end they die unhappy, their ego conquered by the intelligence of nature's inevitable transformation.

Not until people transform from adolescence will they enter the door to adulthood. People who are ready to make the transition to adulthood often experience a midlife crisis. I refer to "midlife crisis" as the early stage of adolescent transformation when we give up acting like an adult and start being an adult. Historically, midlife crises occur in the forties and fifties age range, but the age of those experiencing midlife crises is dropping. People in their twenties or early thirties also can experience a midlife crisis. It is not as obvious, though, because the stakes are usually not as high in terms of lifestyle, career, and family. Typically our parents or caretakers are aging, and we become conscious of their mortality. At this point in our lives we realize we have only been *acting* like adults. The radical change in behavior, typically witnessed during midlife crises, is an attempt to revert to the adolescent years. During this crisis we begin to make more decisions that reflect our inner sense.

Christians often refer to the rediscovery of our inner sense as being "born again." This phrase implies that we allow our ego to die. The Bible says if we (our egos) die, we will get to Heaven. This is probably true because if we aren't living from the ego, we must be living from our inner sense. Realizing Heaven is only possible by living from our inner sense, and adolescent transformation is the rebirth of our inner sense.

Once we become true adults, we let go of the side of the pool and swim on our own. We overcome our fears by confronting them. We stop worrying about other people's opinions of us. We realize that other people's opinions are possibly a reflection of their egos or lack of their own personal resolution. We also refrain from judging others and empathize with their struggle to become free of fears. We better understand our parents and view them in a loving light. We acknowledge and accept the fact that they struggle with the same issues we do. We realize that our parents are the only ones who can assume responsibility for their lives; we don't need to take care of their emotional problems. We also leave old patterns and roles behind and establish a new paradigm for our relation-ships, one of true friendship and compassion. We are free to make our own decisions without protesting or con-forming to our parents' wishes or to those of a social clique. We do not follow the family or peer group unless it is consistent with our essence.

As a result of our increased self-confidence, we perceive the world as a safer place. We are more aware of our sur-roundings and can read people more accurately with a first impression. Because we trust our ability to provide for our-selves, our needs are easily satisfied. We are not afraid to ask for exactly what we want. We are confident and know that we are receiving the energy of a generous world. We nurture ourselves and others because we recognize we are the source of light for others. We remove our mask and let the world see our true inner sense. We feel free and youth-ful because we don't have to act mature — we *are* mature. We learn to play again, not with toys but with our minds. We are more creative because fear of failure is not confining our imagination. Our taste in clothes and music changes as we become open to new ideas and new ways of thinking. Possessions may become less significant as objects to influ-ence the way people perceive us. Instead, our possessions become extensions of our inner sense and provide us with the tools we need to fulfill our purpose. We start to sur-round ourselves with items that bring us enjoyment or con-venience, but not necessarily social acceptance. In effect, we are less ego-oriented and driven. We become less judg-mental and more compassionate.

Personal Integrity

*In the darkness of our past lives we find
the seeds that grow and blossom with
the healing of a wounded heart.*

Personal integrity means we accept full responsibility for defining our essence and then living accordingly. We stay personally aware and immediately adjust our state of being to ensure our compliance with our defined essence. If we are exercising personal integrity, we express our true individualism in our daily lives. We challenge our integrity when our essence causes us to confront our old beliefs or habits. When we are within our integrity, we are less likely to feel the need to conform if something is contrary to our essence. We adjust our daily routine to accommodate our emotional and physical needs. We understand our bodies and listen to what they need. We nurture ourselves continuously. We operate from a position of confidence and trust that our needs will be met. We are not dependent on other people or relationships for our survival, but, instead, interact with others for mutual enrichment. Because we are more trusting, we do not take our careers or jobs too seriously. We do not compromise our values to ensure our popularity or wealth; we don't have to prove anything to anyone. Our creativity and sense of adventure are heightened. We do not try to change other people but accept them as they are, knowing they must learn from their own crises. Still, we are willing to coach those who are asking for direction in their lives. Our expectations and our disappointments are few. We stop blaming other people for the things in our lives we don't like. We know we can make choices to create whatever we want in our lives. Life is not a game we win; we live for the joy of our experiences.

When we start to live with integrity, we feel empowered to create the life we want and we begin to live without fear. Integrity is a statement of self-respect, a commitment to live according to the values defined in our essence.

Chapter 4

≡ Spiritual Development

Internal Orientation

*Life's answers are revealed
to the peaceful mind.*

When we stop working to preserve our ego's image of ourselves, we find that we are internally oriented. Knowing our inner sense feels safe and peaceful; it reminds us of our mother's nurturing ways. The difference is that we find we can nurture ourselves and experience the same level of comfort in our daily lives. That comfort comes from our surroundings and is in our being. We stop struggling and resisting our circumstances. If we feel sick or depressed, we don't have to fix ourselves. We accept that we are in a constant state of transformation. We know we possess the healing power of our inner sense. We know that where we are is where we are meant to be, and that who we are is who we are meant to be at every moment. We do not feel the urge to look for answers outside ourselves. We can trust our inner sense. We are our own therapist and doctor. We have the answers we need when we embrace the power of self-healing.

Because our inner sense connects with nature's energy, we now understand the relationships between ourselves and the people, things, events, and thoughts in our lives. We spend time in silence so that we can listen to our inner sense. We learn to appreciate the beauty and healing powers of nature around us. We are more appreciative of clouds, trees, flowers, rain, sunrise, and sunsets; nature is more rewarding because we recognize our connection to these things. We are more observant and interested in environmental and personal health issues.

Although it may not yet be present in physical form, our vision of the life we want converts to reality through our thoughts, emotions, and behavior. Ironically, the more we experience our essence emotionally, the greater possibility we have to experience our essence in our preferred physical form. For instance, we may live in geographic area with few hills and no trees. Using our inner sense we can experience living in a more scenic environment (without being there physically). When we create this type of realism emotionally, our chances of getting what we want in a physical sense increase.

Inner Peace

The vibration of silence
creates beautiful thoughts.

Inner peace is living life with purpose and fulfilling our essence. A constant state of inner peace is difficult to maintain. However, as we develop an understanding of our essence, we increase the percentage of time we spend living with inner peace. To enjoy the state of inner peace, we must stay immune to the will of the ego.

Inner peace is not about running away to find ourselves but about experiencing the essence of what we want without changing our physical environments. We experience inner peace when we create the life we want out of a situation that we previously thought was impossible to handle. Inner peace feels as though life requires no extra effort. Therefore, we drop the word "work" from our vocabulary. Nothing is work because we choose to participate freely and in a loving way. We do not have to resist the external world around us but embrace it as an acknowledgment of the progress we have made toward fulfilling our essence. We experience a life with a new perspective that makes up a safe and peaceful existence. We relieve ourselves of anxiety related to time. Things happen when they do, not when they should. We can accept that life is a rite of passage. We follow our inner sense and stay focused on our essence. This is where we find fulfillment and happiness.

Harmony with Nature

*Gently touch the tree
and it will touch you back.*

As the percentage of time we spend in a state of inner peace increases, the more aware we become of our powers to communicate and to influence the world in ways once unknown to us. We learn that we can alter energy around us. We learn to help others, using our mental energy like we use an arm or a hand. We access our ability to communicate with energy in all of its forms. Not only do we now understand our purpose in life, but we also know how to fulfill our purpose because we embrace the tools we possess as humans.

Consider the human brain as a source of electrical energy. The frequency at which electricity modulates in the brain depends on our state of mind. We also know that electricity is one method of transmitting energy. Radio and television use electricity to send and receive information that we understand and can use. In very much the same fashion, the human mind can change its electrical energy and frequency to communicate with or influence other forms of energy. This process of communicating is, therefore, not based on the traditional audible or visual methods. The best description of this process is the transference of energy.

The ability to transfer energy derives from our inner sense, which is energy in its purest form since it transforms at its own pace. Unlike the ego, we don't have to control anything in the realm of our inner sense; we totally surrender to our being. When we are in a state of harmony with nature, we can transfer our energy in nonphysical ways but with results that manifest themselves in a physical state. We can, for example, help heal plants, animals, relationships, and people.

Let me further explain how transference can happen: When we are feeling emotionally connected, we can transfer our nurturing, healing, and loving energy to another subject or object. To begin the transference process, we must first experience inner peace. We must recognize our capacity for love, understanding, and compassion. From this loving orientation our transference powers can be exercised. Next, we can change the frequency of our brain waves. This means we feel as one with the object we want to communicate with. We become emotionally connected. We are attuned to its energy modulation or frequency. This establishes the interface or channel for the transference to take place. This process is similar to jump-starting a car with battery cables. However, in this case, we must stay highly focused on our capacity to love, heal, and feel compassionate.

This type of communication is only effective when we are living from our essence. In other words, we cannot use transference to our benefit if our purpose is material acquisition or satisfaction of ego. We will lose our power if we allow the ego to interfere. This process of transference is the basis for the true psychic ability that allows us to communicate via telepathy. This is a highly controversial topic for ego-based people, who confine themselves to the world of physical being. When we are in a harmony with nature, our nonphysical senses are more easily accessible. When we can accept the possibilities that exist beyond what we believe today, we can discover the knowledge of the universe. You will be amazed at how transference works!

Acceptance

He who opens the flower with his thoughts
has the power of the universe.

When we are in harmony with nature, we feel one with the universe, and our existence becomes eternal. We recognize that the universe is in perfect balance at all times, even if it appears we are destroying ourselves. We accept that human life is also a transformation process and that ego imposes many of our perceptions of reality. Once inner sense replaces the ego, the human form can exist without fear in a state of inner peace.

Fear is the source of worry, worry the source of discontent, and discontent the source of crisis. By eliminating fear, the human experience becomes significantly more enriching because of the personal freedom it provides. Ego-based people will use money and other material possessions as a liberation from fear, expecting that their materialism will provide the personal security and freedom they seek. Interestingly enough, the possessions and money often become the enslaving objects, as we strive to maintain and protect them. When we overvalue our human form, it is easy to become entrapped by fear. If we can truly live by our inner sense, we are inherently protecting our being, not our ego or money or objects. This is the challenge of acceptance. Most importantly, it is how we discover our purpose in life and how to fulfill that purpose. The inner sense of the universe guides our energy through the creation and transformation of humanity. Let's learn to enjoy it!

We must develop emotionally
if we want to recognize our spirit.

Part Two

Self-Limitation

❖   ❖   ❖

Chapter 5

≣ Who Are We?

We laugh and we don't know why
We laugh to be accepted
We laugh to hide our fears
We laugh at the expense of others
We laugh at ourselves in embarrassment
We laugh and it is a disguise
Yet we forget to laugh because we are truly happy

The study of human behavior indicates that we are more alike than we are different. Human beings are very much driven by their emotions. In an attempt to satisfy our emotional desires, we undertake the following activities as children and adults: We educate ourselves on many aspects of life, we develop areas of expertise or knowledge, we become interested in aspects of life where we excel. We feel best about ourselves when we can demonstrate a natural aptitude or when we receive validation from someone else.

Most people have a multitude of talents and interests. If we choose, we can focus on more than one specific career during our lives. Unfortunately, we sometimes become so specialized that we ignore our other abilities, and we become one dimensional. We allow our other talents to wither, discouraged by our failure to meet the standards set by others. We believe it when people tell us we are not "good enough" to be the best. We let go of our interests because we do not receive the validation we would like. In our society there is an overemphasis on winning and being the best, as opposed to valuing the experience we gain from pursuing our desires and interests. At some time during our upbringing, we are exposed to the concept of perfection, a notion that comes from our ego. I have found that "perfect" is a relative term. Who can describe a perfect world? Perfection is only relevant in comparison to our expectations or tangible desires.

Maybe a perfect life is when one lives life to the fullest. But how many people do you know who are actually maximizing their potential? Sometimes life's circumstances cause us to ignore our true interests and desires. We then make excuses why we can't pursue our dreams — like too old, too poor, not the right sex, and other limiting thoughts. When we believe the excuses we create, we often fall short of accomplishing what is possible.

In our fast-paced lives we find ourselves echoing the common excuse that there is not enough time. If we are alive, time is an abundant resource available to us. Unlike food, shelter, and health, time is free; even if we want to buy time, we can't. No one can sell us more time! The dilemma is that we haven't learned how to set priorities and balance our lives. The challenge, then, is to find the balance in our lives that allows us to find more of the time that we thought we never had. Finding more time is only possible by choosing a supportive lifestyle — not a lifestyle that motivates us from a parental, monetary, popular, or material sense, but from our capacity to achieve fulfillment in many aspects of life. If we pursue material wealth, our time will be consumed with activities to satisfy the ego. To feel less of a time constraint, we can view life from the perspective of our *experiences*, not only from the perspective of our *achievements*. We can live every moment with value and appreciation. We soon find we can't waste time because every experience is an achievement. Finding more time is not a goal that makes us more productive or fulfilled. Choosing to spend more time in ways that are consistent with our essence is how we live a fulfilled life.

Unless we spend our time ultimately contributing to the development and progress of others, we find ourselves feeling stuck in life. The benefits from sincere generosity are available to people despite their religious affiliation, nationality, political beliefs, or ethnic heritage. If we only focus on the well-being of our ego, we become frustrated by our own stagnation and never find enough time or money to be satisfied. In our very material world, we have chosen to believe that the person who dies with the most toys is the winner. So we are constantly looking at our neighbors or co-workers to measure our success. The grass, naturally, often looks greener on the other side of the fence. The challenge is not to get to the other side of the fence but to cultivate what's on our own side of the fence. Giving to others (as opposed to just throwing money in their direction) provides an opportunity to broaden our perspective by sharing from the heart and not for ego or tax benefits.

The reason we limit ourselves is because we attach meaning to words and events that may not be accurate. Life is simply an experience. How we interpret those experiences is determined by how invested we are in protecting our ego. Life is sometimes enjoyable and sometimes painful. In either case, it has the same meaning unless we decide otherwise.

As we become more aware of our inner sense, we will experience less pain and learn to welcome the more difficult aspects of life as opportunities for higher education. If we are living from our inner sense, we know there is a greater purpose to our endeavors than satisfying our ego-based desires.

There are no methods for making life perfect that exist outside ourselves. Life is already perfect. If we don't think it is, perhaps it's because our expectations do not reflect an understanding of the laws of nature. The power and energy within our reach is enormous. We need to be scientists experimenting with new theories, attitudes, and beliefs. We can challenge ourselves by contemplating ideas that may seem foreign to us. The more technologically advanced we become the more we realize the possibilities to expand the human mind in nontechnical areas. We can take the time to ask questions about life and be brave enough to welcome change. We have nothing to fear; we are our own best safety net once we learn to trust ourselves. If we can learn to believe in ourselves, we will find another life that we never knew was available to us. Good things happen to us when we learn to deal with the facts and don't attach too much meaning to our interpretation of the facts.

Personality Traits That Limit Us

A map will take you
where someone has already been.

Those of us who live in a state of adult theatrics have not yet reclaimed our inner sense. Therefore, we assume at least one of three following personality traits: conformist, perfectionist, or defeatist. The thoughts and actions of most people fall into one primary category although we usually possess characteristics from one of the other two personality types. Sometimes we show various personality traits in different areas of our lives; someone might be aggressive at work and passive at home, or vice versa. Each of these personality types is a manifestation of a person's ego, and our personality is our behavior script that we believe best ensures our survival. These personality traits are established during our childhood experiences, and we will not begin to recognize our potential until we understand how our personality traits are holding us back from true fulfillment and achievement. Discontentment comes from trying to overcome life's trials and tribulations by assuming any one of these personality types. People with these types of personalities feel a sense of dissatisfaction because they are not living from their inner sense. In their way, people who fit into one of these personality categories are ultimately attempting to feel validation and acceptance from others — they are masking a profound lack of confidence and self-esteem. These personality traits are a reflection of external orientation.

Conformist (Lie Low)

*For those who follow the crowd,
retirement of the mind comes early.*

The most common personality type is the conformist, a person who takes the "backseat" approach to life. Conformists seek emotional safety. Instead of taking responsibility for steering their lives, they become passengers. They have almost no control over their destinies. Unfortunately, many end up somewhere they don't want to be.

But why would some of us not want to be in the driver's seat of our lives? Probably because early in our development we lost our self-confidence, and this loss of confidence keeps us stuck in a world with limited possibilities. Life feels dull and mundane because our lives become routine. Our ego tells us to imitate what we see other people doing, so we take few risks and play it safe. We follow the trends to ensure our social acceptance. We imitate what we hear and see at a young age, and we grow older, continuing to imitate others (adult theatrics). Of course, if we want to avoid responsibility and accountability for our lives, then it is best to believe there is safety in numbers and follow the crowd.

Too many conformists lack the confidence to pursue their dreams because they worry about being judged by others. Conformists make up excuses: " I can't," "I don't have talent," "I don't have time," or "I'm too busy." How can we be too busy to live? Conformists have a fear of success and rejection. They are typically unaware of their creative abilities. Therefore, they buy pictures instead of painting them. They are devoted sports fans instead of athletes. They read books instead of writing them. They watch television and movies instead of creating a more exciting life. They buy prepared foods rather than growing food and cooking it themselves. They listen to concerts instead of playing an instrument. If you think you have talent, don't be a conformist; use your abilities to enjoy life.

Stop doing what you "should"
and start being who you are!

Perfectionist (Overcompensate)

He who drives the straight road turns carelessly.

A conformist with an overinflated ego might best char-
acterize the personality of a perfectionist. The perfectionist,
like the conformist, worries about acceptance within a
social structure and behaves in ways to disguise low self-
esteem or lack of confidence. The perfectionist is typically
more aggressive than the conformist and is, therefore,
proactive about satisfying the needs of the ego by eliminating rejection before it has a chance to arise. In other words,
the perfectionist wants to drive the car because no one else
can drive as well; the perfectionist needs to be in control.

The way the perfectionist attempts to maintain control is
by avoiding the possibility of someone spotting a weakness
or flaw first. Any criticism from others is interpreted as a
statement of rejection because, to the perfectionist, flawed
merchandise is not acceptable. This may explain why the
perfectionist is very self-critical. To avoid criticism from
others, perfectionists attempt to excel in whatever they do,
hoping that the insecurities that lurk within the subconscious will be masked. Often the perfectionist develops
addictions that manifest themselves as self-improvement
obsessions — educational, physical fitness, religious, and
self-help programs. This helps the perfectionist to feel a
sense of superiority and justifies being critical of others.
This, of course, leads to destructive communication patterns
in personal relationships because the perfectionist cannot
easily relinquish control of or accept faults in others.

Perfectionists believe the world revolves around their
standards. This severely limits their thinking in a world
with limitless possibilities. For the perfectionist, practicality
and logic replace intuition and emotion. Therefore, the per-

fectionist judges the world logically, using good and bad, right and wrong as the criteria. Of course, nothing in life fits into these categories until we attach a judgment. Being judgmental is a way of life and leads the perfectionist to become alienated from others. There is very little tolerance, understanding, or compassion for others who are different. This perspective stems from a large reservoir of ego.

The perfectionist has low self-esteem and requires constant validation from others. Therefore, the perfectionist thrives on adulation, understanding, tolerance, and compassion. Ironically, perfectionists find it difficult to reciprocate in kind. Typically, perfectionists are not in touch with their feelings. They are defensive and live in a state of denial of their emotions.

Living primarily from ego places the perfectionist out of harmony with nature because the inner sense is suppressed. Despite all the attempts to live a perfect life, being out of harmony with nature will eventually lead to personal crisis. Often the perfectionist cannot anticipate that a personal crisis is imminent unless receiving negative feedback from others. Again, to the perfectionist this critical feedback is a form of crisis. At the point of crisis, the perfectionist has the opportunity to explore an undiscovered dimension of the human potential, which extends beyond logic. With a wounded ego, the perfectionist will try even harder to recapture the image of perfection. In other words, perfectionists are unaware of the effects of their behavior because they are emotionally shut down, and it is difficult for them to become reacquainted with their feelings. Once the perfectionist admits the need for personal improvement, the road to recovery can be realized more rapidly than with other personality types. Perfectionists are in a good position to incorporate new personal development information because they typically push themselves to maintain perfection. True growth comes when the perfectionist realizes that life is not about perfection but about appreciating nature's diverity and its transformation.

Defeatist (Rebel)

*The sheep of the flock who flock from
the sheep remain a flock of sheep.*

The defeatist, like other personality types, comes in various degrees. The personality known as the defeatist emerges after years of living with negative reinforcement and a fear of success and failure. Because defeatists have low self-image and little self-confidence, they may dissociate from their discomfort by developing self-destructive addictions to relationships or substances. Indeed, low self-esteem is the obstacle that prevents the defeatist from becoming a self-nurturing person who experiences a larger, more rewarding life experience. The defeatist has lost all sense of empowerment and usually works jobs that are not emotionally or financially rewarding. Therefore, the defeatist can be a homeless person on the street or a middle-class person with a corporate job.

Like the conformists and the perfectionists, the defeatists are not in tune with their inner sense. Inner sense implies individuality but defeatists believe they are individuals apart from society. Since the defeatist does not feel validated by merely being a conformist, the defeatist seeks ways to express individuality apart from the group through lifestyle choices. The defeatist receives attention by living unconventionally or counter to the conformist. The defeatist, in an attempt to satisfy the ego, finds ways to be acknowledged by others. The defeatist perceives attention as a sign of worthiness. In truth, the defeatist merely joins a group of nonconformists and begins to conform to that subculture.

Defeatists set unconventional guidelines for success yet are seldom successful in the eyes of their ego, which measures them against others. Subconsciously, the defeatist is undermining the desires of the ego to be successful and accepted by society. The defeatist has bought into the values of mainstream society but is consciously denying acceptance of those values. This conflict in values creates a counterproductive cycle of trying to be accepted but never being acceptable. The conflict is a perfect recipe for an unhappy emotional struggle throughout life. This personality type does not feel it deserves to be happy, and it continues to act out the role of the martyr. Using the disguise of "poor old me," the defeatist learns to manipulate others to get attention and handouts. Defeatists interpret any good fortune resulting from their manipulation as "I am okay," "I am worthy," "I deserved it," or "The world owes me." Defeatists become so accomplished at the manipulation game that they may eventually believe they don't need to work to have their needs met. While others go to work, so does the defeatist, manipulating other people or the social system to get the next handout. In a way, defeatists build self-esteem by proving they are smart enough to manipulate others, therefore feeling in control. Lack of intelligence is not a shortcoming for defeatists, which is why they are so good at manipulating others. Sadly, the defeatist does not comprehend what is possible in life.

Fitting into Society

You will never see the beauty of the stars until you move away from the glitter of artificial lights.

Just as there are laws of nature, society develops rules, policies, and laws to enhance the chances of survival and to improve the quality of life for its members. Further, to provide for its members, society will work to find efficient ways to meet the needs of the mainstream or dominant group. Accomplishing this task is easiest when there is conformity. The group views any individual not willing to conform as a threat and will alienate and discard individuals who do not conform. Since the natural disposition is toward survival, most people choose to conform within the limits of the written or unwritten rules. This is why each of us has at least some degree of conformist in our personality.

Since each personality type discussed previously is a manifestation of our ego, fear of extinction, rejection, and abandonment triggers the personality we feel best guarantees our survival. The fear of pain and death leads us to conform to at least a few social standards. We personally feel threatened if we become rejected by the group or its members. We become obsessed with our need to be accepted. From early childhood, we learn the rules of conformity from the family, church, school, and business. They attempt to tell us how to spend our personal time. That is how we all end up at the football stadium or watching the "big" game on television instead of following our true inner sense. We become clones by taking on the identity of a social group (company, team, political party, ethnic group, religion, gang, state, city, nationality, and the list goes on). The point is that our ego tells us to conform to society so we can feel accepted.

Unfortunately, society teaches us that acceptance is dependent on our success and money is often the key to success. Therefore, most of us believe money leads to success, success leads to acceptance, and acceptance leads to happiness. Following this logic we can conclude that people with material and financial wealth are extraordinarily happy. However, this seems to be a misconception because success has disproportionately little to do with our satisfaction or happiness in life. Those with success struggle with the same problems as those of modest means; they struggle with relationships, finances, health, and job satisfaction.

So why do we strive for wealth in our society when it does not guarantee happiness? The reason is that we constantly look at success and happiness based on external appearances. Then we compare ourselves to others instead of assessing if we are fulfilling our purpose in life. Even the defeatist, who pretends not to care what other people think, measures success by the gifts or handouts received. Of course, those who appear successful and those who appear to be failures seem very different because the primary measurement of success in our society is our financial and material status. Surprisingly, both groups suffer from low self-esteem but choose different personality traits to help cover up their fear of rejection.

Supplementing Our Personalities

Peace of mind is found in a loving heart.

As mentioned earlier, we establish our survival techniques early in life. Few of us want to confront our fears or risk losing the little bit of happiness we have by developing new patterns of behavior. We haven't learned to trust and believe in our inner sense to provide the things we need. What is the real risk? Energy is never destroyed! We are transforming whether we like it or not. Why not enjoy our passage through humanity?

The challenge for most of us is to learn the meaning of love. We often hear people talk about giving love, but how can we give something if we don't know exactly what it is we are being asked to give? Love exists when we let go of our ego because at that point we realize we are in harmony with nature; this is our essence and purpose in life. Since it is not possible to give our inner sense to another person, it is more appropriate to describe love as an act of sharing. To share love means to express the joy of living from our inner sense. We cannot, however, share love without first nurturing and caring for ourselves. As a hit song once suggested, "Learning to love yourself is the greatest love of all." Self-love is the best place to start and to practice love. When we share love we receive it in return.

The biggest thing missing from the ego is Love and Trust. "L" and "T" are the two most important letters removed from the word ego. If we add Love and Trust to our ego, we can LeTgo of the fear that binds us. Love and trust allow us to take the leap of faith necessary to change our old patterns of behavior. When we let go of our ego, we can reclaim our inner sense. Fear is the single biggest limiting factor in most of our lives. Rejection is one of our most prevalent fears. But how can we be rejected from the universe that we belong to and can't escape from? How can energy be rejected or abandoned? We can trust that we can never be rejected because our energy is always at home in the universe. The more we transpose our own internal energy from ego to inner sense, the more we rejuvenate ourselves, and the greater our capacity becomes to share love.

Love is important because it is compassion and understanding that allow us to feel connected to all people and living things. Love helps us to realize we are never alone. Only when we become what we want will we experience what we want. If we want to feel loved, we must be a loving person. If we want honesty, we must be honest. Our lives are a reflection of either our ego or our inner sense. Our level of consciousness determines how we choose to live. Others who are in tune with the same level of consciousness can pick up on the energy we emit; we are like big magnets, attracting or repelling certain events, thoughts, feelings, things, and people. This exchange is an example of energy transference. The transference of loving energy occurs through understanding, compassion, sensitivity, awareness. We must stay open-minded to the possibility that our caring will make a difference. When we experience love we share the comfort of these same qualities. We can transpose negative (angry) energy into a more gentle and peaceful awareness within ourselves.

Love, Trust, and let go of ego!

Chapter 6

≡ The Emotional Trap

How Fear Limits Our Potential

Tomorrow never comes
for those who have not lived today.

The origin of the thoughts that limit us is fear. Fear is an opposing emotion to security. Whether we wish to admit it or not, we each harbor fear. Fear influences our behavior and our behavior helps us to feel more secure or fulfilled. This is why we develop habitual patterns of behavior. The problem is we don't know why we are afraid or when we are acting out of fear, so our subconscious acts on our behalf. We go through life unaware of why we do the things we do. We simply react to our external environment based on our fears. That is why we find ourselves not getting our desires met and concluding that life is unfair. Fear hypnotizes us, and our robotic behavior is dangerous because it limits our potential to experience our essence. Do not forget, we often experience what we are afraid of because we live based on our projections of the future. As an analogy, consider how limited we would be without the use of our thumb. The thumb, although not very big, gives us extreme flexibility to accomplish tasks vital to our survival. To build a house without the use of a thumb would be almost impossible; we could barely hold a hammer or saw. When we succumb to fear it is like losing an emotional thumb. Our fears are disabling us from building a greater life than what we now know. Once fear consumes our thoughts and emotions; the energy we emit changes and the world responds to us differently. We may notice that dogs who sense our fear bark or chase us. If we ignore the dog, it loses interest and goes away. If we approach life with fear, our problems become like the dogs that *chase* us and won't go away.

Fear of Death

The gate to heaven is open to those who enter new dimensions in thought.

Since our transformation (death) is inevitable, why do we resist the thought that we will die? The reason is that most of us fear the unknown. Fear originates at birth when we separate from our mother's womb. This is when we first realize our separateness and individuality. Our attachment to ego keeps us frightened of anything that we believe threatens our existence. We seem to be missing a sense of security, positive self-esteem, and a sense of purpose.

Instead of living with confidence, the media conditions us to believe that our survival is threatened at every turn. I am not suggesting that the events reported on the evening news are not real, but the chances of us dying on any given day are not very great. Although the chances of dying are greater in some situations than in others, most of us are fortunate enough to confront death only once in our lives.

Violence in civilized societies results from low self-esteem. Our level of self-esteem sometimes stems from our abusive cultural conditioning, which is reinforced over multiple generations. Anger is buried in the hearts of those who know the frustration of families, communities, and governments that say to us, "You are nobody." The media perpetuates this hopelessness by continuing to emphasize the importance of fame and material wealth as a form of social acceptance. Too often we measure our self-worth based on the affluence we see displayed on television. When we have low self-esteem, we put ourselves in the position of the victim. Feeling victimized for long periods of time can lead to intense anger. We act out our anger aggressively by abusing others in varying degrees. When violence entraps a particular community for multiple generations, a subculture evolves. For decades, violent cultures have evolved worldwide where religious, national, or ethnic oppression has been a way of life.

When we feel threatened with a life-or-death situation, we give up our individuality and try to find safety in the crowd. Conformity is one method of camouflage that helps to keep us from standing out. Even zebras herd together to avoid the dangers of an attacking lion because the many stripes confuse the predator who tries to single out a potential victim. After many years of social abuse, the pressure to conform is in the minds of those who have been victims of violence, prejudice, and discrimination. Even after the atrocities of our anger subside, the next generation has already witnessed the events and learned to place blame for our suffering on others. The fear of death or abuse remains, though the names and places change. We stay attached to our personal and family history, which suggests that someone is out to persecute us. Thus we remain victims, sometimes for a lifetime. Living from our history is a form of self-inflicted oppression. Oppression of any sort generally leads to anger, which is then expressed through aggressive and violent behavior.

There is very little psychological difference between the oppressed and the oppressor. They are both victims and respond to the world in the best way they know how. The oppressed person chooses to conform to remain inconspicuous while the oppressor acts from fear of retaliation and survival. "Get them before they get you" is the motto of the survivor. Our fears of becoming a victim lead us to become a victim of our fears.

We have a choice not to fear death. If we can believe that our death is not the end of our existence but a transformation of our energy, we can begin to overcome our fears. No human being can kill another human; we can only kill the ego. Spirit is eternal for it lives in the minds of those who have been recipients of our being. True greatness is when people get over our deaths but don't get over our lives.

Fear of Pain

Pain is the friend of resistance and
the foe of those who yield to it.

After the fear of dying, the fear of pain is a prominent one in the human psyche. Pain is the transference of negative energy to the central nervous system. Thus, pain can be experienced either physically or emotionally. Most of us try to avoid pain. Like our fear of death, pain causes us to modify our behavior. Pain is most commonly caused by an imbalance in one's life — that is to say, when we are not living according to our inner sense. As a result, our emotional pain manifests itself as a physical ailment or disease. Another source of pain is that inflicted by an external source. For example, we become involved in an accident that is not our fault. External pain is a result of not being aware of our external environment as it relates to our inner sense. If we are aware of our inner sense and living according to our essence, we can avoid accidents that aren't our fault. Accidents happen to help us gain greater awareness of our inner sense. Therefore, the benefit of pain is that it helps to break down our ego.

Because most of us are unaware of our internal being, we have generally developed our awareness about our external surroundings from our families, the media, and our own experiences (our interpretations of reality). If we are living from our inner sense, we inherently know when we are in harmony with nature. Being in harmony boosts our immunity to the dangers that await us in the world of the human ego. Living without personal conflict is an insurance policy we can issue to ourselves. The premium we have to pay is the belief that our energy cannot be destroyed.

Fear of Rejection and Abandonment

Ego, the basis of pride, prevents us
from recognizing the freedom of choice
to improve our condition.

Pain also stems from loneliness, which is an emotion caused by feeling rejected or abandoned by others. Our fears of emotional pain are what keep us from experiencing the joy of relationships with other people. Emotions ruled by our ego can wreak havoc in our personal lives without our even knowing it. Depending on our personal level of confidence and self-esteem, we are more or less susceptible to behaviors and decisions that help us avoid rejection. When we deny our fears, we eventually see the effects manifested in various ways. Fear of rejection drives us to make choices that limit our potential fulfillment. This means we avoid finding new relationships, livelihoods, or lifestyles. Instead, we avoid taking action to create the life we really want.

Perhaps there are other approaches to dealing with our emotions. Some cultures express emotions with passion but without threatening their relationships. This type of expression is a sign of being alive and of mutual respect. For example, in some cultures it is acceptable to have differing opinions and not alienate others. Debates surrounding differences in opinion are a sign of intellect and not necessarily conflict. After work it is possible to ignore previous disagreements and still be genuinely sociable with a philosophical opponent. In some countries disagreements are discussed without causing the opposition to lose "face." In other words, we can debate the issue without degrading the other person. This is a constructive way to express ourselves without feeling judged or threatened. Many relationships could benefit if we learned that conflict does not mean we are not likable human beings. The emphasis on popularity in some cultures causes us to spend too much of our time trying to figure out how we can convince people to accept us.

Fear and Addiction

A mind consumed with the ego
fails to nurture the soul.

We carry our fears with us from childhood into the adult theatrics phase of our development. We typically do not confront our fears. Instead, we find distractions to make ourselves feel better so we don't have to deal with pain and rejection. This is the perfect setup for the development of obsessive or compulsive behavior. We cling to activities that make us feel good or allow us to dissociate from our fears. These activities include drinking, smoking, taking drugs, eating, gambling, abusing others, abusing ourselves, pursuing sexual gratification and relationships, exercising, shopping, cleaning, working, and the list continues. Our lives become routine and boring as we lose our spontaneity and our behavior becomes predictable. Until we deal with our fears, we will be habitually consumed in one or more compulsive behaviors.

When an activity becomes an addiction, then our lives become unbalanced, the body's immune system weakens, and we become more susceptible to illness and depression. It is the mind that controls the body; however, when we become addicts, our minds fall out of touch with the needs of our bodies. The result is we don't get enough rest, we don't eat healthfully, or we leave ourselves exposed to accidents.

You can never run from your past,
you can only be aware of its influence
in the present moment.

If we want to break our destructive or addictive patterns of behavior, we must first understand our fears. Locating the source of our fears is the best place to start. When we identify the source of fear as ego, we recognize the role addictions play in protecting our ego, we figure out what we really want in life, and we emotionally let go of the material objects and activities that we use to satisfy our ego. Therefore, we need to let go of the things we are doing to make ourselves feel better. We feel best when the mind and body learn to work in harmony to become one. (Caution: Regular physical exercise does not mean that we are in harmony with our mental energy.) When we allow ourselves permission to be who we are from our inner sense, then we discover our essence.

Attitudes That Limit Our Potential

You can never measure results
in a changing world.

Attitudes are habitual patterns of thought and serve to shape our behavior. Attitudes toward life come from our interactions with the external world. We adopt attitudes based on our experiences or from someone else's point of view. Attitudes that are based on negative experiences can limit us because we are predestined to repeat those experiences in our minds when we are reminded of the past. In these situations, we become victims of our fear and our projections of what the future will be like. On the other hand, if we are influenced by someone else, our attitude normally causes us to accept other people's reality as our own. In this scenario, we also have a tendency to prejudge events or people, and this leads us be closed-minded to possibilities. Being unable to see possibilities often causes us to blame other people for our problems. Again, this places us in the role of the victim because we have no basis for interpreting reality, especially if we use gossip or conjecture as the basis.

Additionally, attitudes also stem from the denial of our emotions. The difference between an emotion and an attitude is that an emotion is spontaneous while an attitude is a premeditated response to a series of past emotions designed to protect the ego. For example, one partner who is interested in ending a relationship approaches the other with the proposal to break up. The recipient of the idea may feel rejected. However, while not acknowledging the emotions, the recipient develops an attitude that helps to cope with the situation. Instead of describing the emotion the person may say, "It doesn't matter," or "I don't care, it wasn't a good relationship anyway," and other excuses that help to ignore true feelings.

The attitudes that are most limiting to us are those that do not nurture us or others. We limit ourselves when we demonstrate a loss of compassion for other energy forms. Sometimes our attitudes can be self-destructive. Hate-based attitudes are most often just a reflection of how we feel about ourselves. Due to our low self-esteem, we find it easier to blame others than to deal with our fears of inadequacy. In an attempt to protect our ego, we cast the disapproval of ourselves onto others. This is not unusual when we don't know our essence.

One might ask why it is that hateful people really dislike themselves. Often it is because, as children, we were abused. We then express our residual anger and low self-esteem by adopting an attitude that assumes the world would be better off if it weren't for "those other people." By placing the blame for our discontent on someone else, we actually become the victim. If we are hateful, we give away our personal power to create the essence of what we really want (to feel good about ourselves). What we can conclude is that we are victims of past abuse and want to express our frustration. Like most people, those of us filled with hate seek acknowledgment, approval, and acceptance. This means most of us who have not discovered our essence still harbor judgments and prejudices toward others.

We need to have a healthy attitude about ourselves. If we don't discover our inner sense, we usually imitate the behavior and assume the beliefs of those ego-based people whom we respect. Sometimes we give away our personal power by taking on the attitude of our role models. The role model is one of the most psychologically damaging inventions to be introduced in modern times. Role models appeal to our ego but offer little encouragement to our individuality. Role modeling promotes adult theatrics, which is like a stage production: The cast listens to the director who decides how to play the roles more convincingly. Unfortunately, a stage play is exactly that, whereas our lives are an experience in which we can choose our roles and act the parts, not as someone tells us to, but as we would like to create it. We set our own criteria for success based on the essence of our desires and not on the form, which is all that a role model can offer. By selecting other people as role models, we may ignore living from our essence. The challenge is to distinguish our desires from those given to us by someone else. We have yet to learn that self-respect is the best role model. So we aspire to be like someone else instead of being who we are.

Chapter 7

Interactions

Relationships That Trap Us

First the unspoken expectations
Then the action
Followed by perception
Made real by interpretation
Ahead the vehicle of communication
Awaits clarity in the form of honesty
A new reality emerges from the fog
The beacon from the lighthouse
Welcomes the experienced sailor
Back home to the shores of love.

Fear and self-esteem are key factors that determine the types of relationships we develop. The relationships that we encounter are a result of our subconscious needs to resolve feelings of rejection, pain, or possibly death. We often have a tendency to cling to relationships because of our sense of responsibility, but more importantly because we fear loneliness. However, we seldom process these feelings consciously.

When we try to avoid emotional discomfort, we cannot express ourselves openly and honestly, and so relationships take on a very superficial character. In our intimate relationships we often do not express our emotions openly. Typically, one person will compromise to avoid a confrontation, or another person may become very controlling and domineering. This aggressive behavior is really an attempt to keep the partner from leaving in hopes that rejection or abandonment can be avoided. Every relationship requires concessions to be made by each partner at various times; however, these concessions are detrimental if either partner compromises his or her essence.

Most of us place too much responsibility on others for determining the quality of relationships we have; we don't accept responsibility for the people we bring into our lives or how we treat them. If we become unhappy, we simply dissolve the relationship and usually blame the other person. The point is we need to develop relationships with people who are aligned with our essence. Instead we usually live as if life were a dance. We find new partners who know the old steps and who follow our lead. This dance keeps us from letting go and expressing ourselves in true individual form. We worry too much about what our dance partners and what the spectators might think. (How often have you ever danced alone in public?) This is especially true as we become stuck in the phase of adult theatrics. Our fears create situations and bring people in our lives that keep us confined to old behavior. A crisis can sometimes be the catalyst to have us explore what has caused us pain in our lives or relationships.

In the final analysis, we need to observe not how others treat us, but how we treat ourselves. Self-exploration allows us to attract relationships that align with our essence.

Family

The mind sometimes acts as a dam,
holding back the flow of the heart.

For most of us, the single greatest asset and detriment to personal development is the family. Our family environment gives us an initial image of what life is and how we will respond to it. Family experiences and the observations of our parents' and siblings' behaviors determine if our disposition toward life will be trusting, fearful, loving, angry, freeing, restricting, accepting, or judgmental. Families can pass on their life orientation and belief systems for generations. One common belief is that traditions must be maintained. Often, traditions serve to impede the evolution of the inner sense. Despite our ethnic or cultural background, each family is carrying some limitations introduced by the last generation. We believe that because our families survived doing things the old-fashioned way, it must be the best way. This thinking never considers that there may be a healthier and more rewarding alternative.

Today there is much focus on the dysfunctional family. So much so that it has left some individuals "stuck" and asking, "Why me? Why can't I be from a normal family?" Many have literally become bogged down and immobilized by the notion of being from a dysfunctional family; they live the label while seeking to blame their families for their difficulties in life. When we think about it, dysfunction is nothing more than another family tradition. The dysfunctional tradition may be that the family does not allow its members to follow their inner sense. Instead, fear subconsciously consumes the primary caretakers or parents. They then impose their fears, unrequited dreams, or unresolved frustrations on their offspring during childhood. As family roles develop to accommodate these fears and desires, the relationships become stunted and the children become extensions of their parents' ego and fear. As everyone scrambles to be validated, alliances develop that cause relationships to develop, not independently, but with conditions for acceptance. Each person's inner sense becomes further suppressed.

Family roles help to add perceived stability to the family dynamic. If we subscribe to the roles we assumed during childhood, we typically ensure our acceptance by the family. The thing that keeps most of us aligned with our family role is the fear of rejection by the family. Each member knows what behavior will solicit a particular reaction from another. We use this knowledge to push another person's buttons; it is a form of indirect control and communication. Once we find a behavioral formula that works in the family environment, we tend to avoid changing. We continue to act out the roles that we assume for ourselves. The family also knows how to push our buttons and, in this way, controls us. But when we reach adolescence, we believe we can make our own decisions and know what is in our best interest. So, in our quest of independence, we decide to challenge the family behavior model.

In most instances, families reject those members who attempt to change their roles. Changing roles creates conflicts that primarily surround the need for each member to fulfill his or her ego. Of course, everyone wants to believe they are right. The parent wants to maintain control and the adolescent wants respect. The family tries to maintain its dynamic by keeping the co-dependent relationships intact.

The family member who deviates from the prescribed value formula may fear being disowned or alienated. Indeed, those who have the courage to venture off to explore a new world of possibilities will experience an initial negative reaction and lack of support from some family members. (After all, they are breaking tradition!) Each of us seeking independence from old family roles must persevere and have confidence that the family, despite short-term ridicule, will again accept its more courageous members. Often, those who are most critical of our actions often respect us for doing what they cannot. Some of us may already feel distance from our families while others may feel extreme closeness. Closeness also limits us because it might mean we are enmeshed with the egos of other family members. In either case, we can learn to let go of past feelings that may have kept us apart or overinvolved with our families.

Those of us who lack the pioneering spirit choose to live with self-imposed limitations. We, therefore, do not consider relocating, new career opportunities, or quality relationships that might improve our lives. Most of all, we restrict our sense of freedom. This form of self-oppression is keeping many people from recognizing their true potential.

The family is just a group of individuals who collectively struggle through life. Families evolve based on tradition and personalities that together establish family values. For example, many families orient themselves toward "doing" things; it is their tradition. Few families experience "being" together without *doing* something together. Also, family values are sometimes based on activities (birthdays, holidays, weddings, and other special events) and how they are carried out. To improve our family relationships, we must first let go of our egos so that we can improve the quality of communication. We also need to recognize how our families have influenced and are continuing to influence the limits we place on ourselves. We need to be aware of the family beliefs that create limitations or possibilities in our minds.

We can learn to diminish the impact our families have on our happiness and fulfillment by choosing to break tradition. We can choose to decide what we want in life. The result can be an acceptance of our parents as they are and a realization that they have done the best they could as parents. Knowing our essence is the key to staying honest in this challenge. Our inner sense is not dependent on the ego of other family members. Choosing to break tradition and to follow our inner sense can lead us to a life filled with possibilities, miracles, and the magic that comes with minimal effort.

Friends

Life sometimes rewards us with friendship that reflects the beauty of our own tranquility.

We are responsible for the relationships we attract in our lives. In our ego-based world, we seek to find acceptance from those we call our friends. Often the people we bring into our lives are a reflection of our need to fill the void left by our family relationships. Friendship means different things to different people. A friend is sometimes an acquaintance with whom we have positive contact. For others, a friend is someone who is willing to sustain an intimate relationship without feeling judged or rejected. In terms of developing quality relationships, we don't need to differentiate between family and those outside the family. Our genetic relationship to someone does not inherently improve or worsen the quality of our relationship with that person.

We can decide what qualities we want in our friendships. Generally, we seek compassion, understanding, honesty, and open communication. The most personally rewarding friendships are those that allow honesty and trust to abound. This is only possible when judgment of the other person is absent.

Relationships are not always balanced. But in a healthy friendship, neither party is keeping score on calls, gifts, or frequency of interaction. True friendship goes beyond doing things together and enters a spiritual realm where communication extends beyond the physical connection. Sometimes we may feel we are not contributing equally to the relationship because we cannot give as much as we receive. Every relationship involves a transfer of energy. The party that shares openly in the relationship and helps a friend become self-aware also benefits. The sharing parties have a chance to rehearse and reinforce elements of personal development fitting to themselves. This lets the sharing person stay conscious and self-aware. By increasing the amount of time we spend in a state of self-awareness, it will be easier to stay true to our inner sense. As we mature and discover our inner sense, we help our friends evolve emotionally or let them go to find their path to satisfaction and fulfillment. We eventually learn to recognize where our friends are in their personal development cycle. Those friendships that allow us to experience our essence are healthy relationships and can usually help us to develop emotionally and spiritually, and to be honest with ourselves.

Work Environment

*The only true competition in life is yourself,
everyone else is here to help you realize it.*

Often our work environment determines how we develop relationships on the job. In most job environments there exists a distinct work culture. Work culture determines how easy it will be for us to dissociate from our ego. In very politically-oriented environments, it is more difficult to divorce one's ego from the environment. If we are ego-invested and require acceptance from others, we limit our potential by playing the political game. A political or bureaucratic work environment is evidence of a fear-based culture. This type of work culture can easily manipulate employees by preying on their insecurities.

Conflict arises when we encounter co-workers with a personal agenda designed to satisfy their egos — without regard for the well-being of others or the business. Managers who meet this description are less effective leaders when their primary concern is their survival or advancement. Unfortunately, many companies promote employees who fit a personality model instead of those who offer the best performance or stimulation. The result is often employees and managers who demonstrate poor judgment, communication, organizational efficiency, productivity, employee morale, and problem solving skill, clearly a recipe for declining profits.

Since we spend most of our days at our place of employment, it easy to see how we can become influenced by the energy of those with whom we work. Work relationships are very similar to family relationships in that we don't always get to select our co-workers. We are sometimes fortunate enough to develop friendships on the job. However, in some situations, we find we work with people who do not share our values or personal priorities. If their energy carries a strong ego-based content, then it becomes difficult to maintain our inner sense. We can be sucked into the politics and become dissatisfied with our job. Usually, we are unaware of how we enter this unhappy state. Like a large, invisible spider web waiting to catch its unsuspecting prey, our ego traps us, making it difficult for us to regain a healthy perspective on work and even life.

Unfortunately, if we have a large ego investment in our success, we risk our mental and physical health and also the health of others. We work overtime to maintain our image as a model employee, manager, or executive. We allow our ego to become involved in a struggle for acceptance as we strive to perform our duties and get ahead financially.

Some criminals also share a similar enthusiasm for financial success. Criminals understand when they break the law but feel the rewards are worth the risk of getting caught. The criminal may also harm others during the crime. This need for immediate gratification shows little concern for harmonious living. Like criminals, many of us define success one-dimensionally. In western society, money is synonymous with success. Focusing on material success causes us to lose sight of the balance that is important to our physical and mental health. We are out of balance when we fail to nurture our souls with love, compassion, and sharing. It seems the more our attention is on success, the greater the chances are of experiencing personal crisis. We eventually lose our capacity to handle challenging circumstances effectively because our focus is on satisfying our ego. We become so consumed with satisfying our ego that we create stress that comes from our fears of failure. Ultimately, too much stress keeps us from meeting the financial or material objectives that we associate with success.

Living to satisfy one's ego ultimately leads to crisis. This crisis may be in our relationships, in our personal health, or in our emotional well-being. Through crisis is the only way many of us come to learn about our essence. However, when we broaden our definition of success, we become more balanced in our thoughts, emotions, and in selecting our priorities.

Following our inner sense is easiest when we give up

our career aspirations and focus on our purpose. This means our success in not measured in terms of external rewards but in terms of self-discovery and inner peace. Those who follow their inner sense and understand the essence of their desires experience well-rounded success. If we understand our purpose in life, our place of employment is an ideal environment for us to make a difference in the lives of others. In a healthy work environment and through healthy work relationships, we can establish quality friendships. We can help our friends with personal issues, encouraging their creativity and self-esteem. Also, we enjoy our days more with this kind of interaction. Ultimately, the business benefits from happier and more productive employees.

Partners

True love can only be discovered
by those who are pioneers of the soul;
you must search the darkness
and there you will find the light.

From the time we reach adolescence we seek to have more sexually intimate relationships; we want to experience exclusivity in a primary relationship. This is partly a result of the natural maturing process but also an attempt at adult theatrics. From childhood we learn that being adult means getting married, having a family, respectable employment, and financial security. It also means that others accept us more readily if we conform to these ideals. To capitalize on this mind-set, we use appearance, wealth, popularity, talent, and sex as vehicles for attracting people to us. The natural development of one's sexuality cannot be denied. However, combining sexuality and ego distorts our perspective about relationships. Relationships guided by individual insecurities, societal definitions, and judgments limit our potential for joy.

Adult theatrics are often prevalent when we enter relationships looking for a permanent mate. This type of adolescent relationship lacks an understanding of each person's essence. During our teenage years, many of us have no clue what we want in our lives. Acceptance and validation are important to our self-esteem. Unfortunately, it is during this time that we maintain certain patterns of behavior designed to validate us among family and friends. We carry these patterns with us into physical adulthood. Continuing in the same role as when we are younger doesn't allow us to overcome our insecurities. We seldom choose a partner based on our own strengths but instead select our partners based on traditional family roles.

Often we are attracted to our partners based on appearances only. The media defines our perception of beauty. We become infatuated with the images of perfection, whether they are people, cars, houses, clothes, or jewelry. If it helps us improve our image, we fall in love with it. Models chosen by the media set the standard by which others measure our appearance. The closer we match that image the more acceptable we believe we are. People spend much time and money fantasizing and trying to perfect that media look. If we can't look like a "media perfect person," then the next best thing is to find a partner who most closely resembles the image of perfection. When we become infatuated, we are also obsessed and our ego begins to imagine what it would be like if we were with the perfect mate. This illusion of finding the perfect mate is a trap for many people because almost no one is good enough to match the fabricated image presented to us by the media. Yet we believe if we find the perfect match, we will feel happy and in a state of perpetual bliss. The fallacy, similar to the idea that material wealth brings happiness, is that physical beauty equates with perfection.

In other words, we have a tendency to select our partners as a crutch to compensate for our shortcomings and lack of self-confidence. Consequently, the criteria we use for choosing a partner may not be in our best interest. In a way, it is the equivalent of putting two incomplete people together. The reason this type of relationship is personally limiting is because it sets up an unhealthy dependence between the partners. This type of codependent relationship does not provide fertile ground for conscious personal development.

Codependent relationships eventually experience conflict surrounding issues that may not have been obvious during the infatuation or even courting period of a relationship. These issues can sometimes lay dormant for years because neither partner is aware of what he or she really wants. If one partner explores personal growth opportunities, the change can threaten the relationship with separation. Unfortunately, we don't always have the insight to know what is most important to building healthy relationships. We somehow imagine ourselves with a person who possesses that flawless image, but we give little consideration to the quality of the relationship we would like to have with that person.

Our infatuation with perfection often leads us into empty relationships that lack depth, honesty, and integrity, the very ingredients needed to support a quality partnership. Yet because of low self-esteem, many of us who don't feel we deserve a perfect mate settle for the person we feel will simply accept us. This approach can also cause us to be unhappy in our relationships because we accept the standards set by the media but realize we can't match the standard.

Many relationships end because people believe they can find a better relationship with another partner. While this is sometimes true, even the new relationship will eventually be laced with its share of difficulties unless our focus is on the essence of living in harmony. This places much more responsibility on each individual to stay personally aware.

The person who seeks to have maximum fulfillment and harmony will avoid unhealthy relationships. An emotionally healthy person prefers to experience life with a partner who shares the same purpose or essence. To experience a relationship based on essence, as opposed to codependency, is to know the meaning of love, trust, and the feeling of freedom. Together with our partners we share a oneness with the energy of life.

True friendship is an integral part of healthy relationships. We feel less insecure about ourselves and our relationships. These relationships are just another gift of nature for us to enjoy but come with no guarantees; they are seldom free of confrontation or trials and tribulations. However, our relationships will have the facility and the communication skills to maneuver through challenging times more easily. We don't have to deal with the fear of losing the relationship.

The key to healthy relationships is our ability to be compassionate, gentle, patient, kind, and nurturing. Each partner must avoid judging the relationship as good or bad, right or wrong. The primary focus for each partner is on maintaining inner peace in the relationship. By accepting the challenge of personal development, we also develop compassion and respect for the road on which our partners are traveling. We can live with these qualities once we let go of our egos and become more loving and trusting. We can eliminate jealousy when we trust ourselves.

If our focus is on our essence, it matters very little with whom we share our lives. After we become comfortable with loving ourselves, we then find that we can establish and share many relationships simultaneously that align with our essence. Each relationship finds its level of depth without anyone trying to steer it. If we live from our inner sense, we don't need to define or categorize our relationships as friends, lovers, acquaintances, family, or any other terms we use; we can treat everyone consistently and equally.

Love is not about the object that we love but is a reflection of how we feel about ourselves. Once we understand this, we discover that the special someone in our lives exists in everyone we meet and every living thing we interact with. When we can recognize this possibility, we experience the essence of what we want in life. The best relationships are those shared by two individuals who truly understand their state of being.

Marriage vows ask us to promise to do things like cherish, hold, look after in sickness and in health, and so on. We are ready for marriage when we can honestly say to our mates, "I am," instead of "I do." We learn that we have most to share when we are in a state of being and not in a state of doing. Many couples perceive their relationships as requiring much effort. It feels like effort because they are constantly under demands to "do" things. We need to learn how to just "be" with one another. We need to be accepting of ourselves and of our partner. Comparing our partners and relationships with others will distract us from creating the relationships we want. We need to stay focused on the essence of the relationship that we and our partners want. As long as we stay focused on our essence, our thoughts and actions will always support and lead us in the direction of the life we wish to experience. We must be the person that we want our partners to be. This is the responsibility of each individual who seeks a satisfying relationship filled with freedom, acceptance, love, and trust.

THE FIVE COMPONENTS
OF A HEALTHY RELATIONSHIP

(1) LEARN TO LOVE YOURSELF

This means becoming an adult, discarding family expectations and childhood fears. It means taking care of your physical and emotional needs. It means learning to trust yourself.

(2) LEARN TO COMMUNICATE

This means overcoming your fear of confrontation so that you can feel comfortable expressing your own opinions, thoughts, and feelings. It also means learning to listen not only to others but to yourself.

(3) LEARN TO BE CONSIDERATE

This means being aware of the cause and effect of your actions. It means listening and understanding others. It means being compassionate, empathetic, and sensitive to others.

(4) LEARN TO ACCEPT OTHERS AS THEY ARE

This means not trying to change others into the image that you want them to be. It means giving them guidance and encouragement to recognize their potential as a truly loving person.

(5) LEARN TO FACILITATE AWARENESS

This means being open-minded and enthusiastic about new ideas, experiences, and thoughts. It means viewing the trials and tribulations of daily life as an opportunity for personal development and self-discovery. It means taking risks with the confidence that your journey will be enhanced.

Ego and Sex

The thorn of a rose never attacks the observer.

Sex is a most confusing and overdiscussed topic in our lives. Historically, society has told us through churches, social morals, and laws that sex is bad. While not all societies think this way, premarital sex has been frowned upon in many religious cultures. By contrast, modern society through the media (on television, at the movies, and on the billboards along the highway) tells us sex is good. So which is it, good or bad? From adolescence to adulthood we are never really sure, so we make up rules that we believe work for us. Unknowingly, we remain confused by the role of sex in our lives. Underlying our sexuality is the ego, waiting secretly in the background for someone to tell us we are attractive, and, more importantly, acceptable and lovable.

The functional aspect of sex is that it serves to procreate the species or human energy form. If we were truly living from our inner sense, we would conceive children in love and in harmony. Many of us, instead, conform to the expectations of our families or society. Sometimes we believe people will accept us as mature adults if we are parents. For many, the idea of having children is a way to leave a legacy to the world. For others, it is an opportunity to live vicariously through their children and to get a second chance in life by fulfilling their unrequited dreams. Still others have children to feel closer to their partners by using the children as a common bond. Lastly, people have children in an attempt to feel unconditional love, which means we are back to satisfying the ego.

When taken out of the context of "society," sex is really no different from any other pleasure we experience in life. Sex provides another way to dissociate from our emotional

wounds by satisfying our ego (in a fantasy or in our perception of reality). We understand this best when we realize that the mind controls the body. As humans, we use sex
for physical pleasure and to fill our emotional voids.

Each of us appreciates validation because it helps us to
overcome the insecurities inflicted by our ego. During sex
we sometimes come close to our inner sense. After a sexual
encounter, many of us feel a closeness or a bond. This is
a good example of how inner sense can bring us closer to
living life in harmony with energy or nature. What most of
us don't realize is that this type of bond and closeness is
available to us on a daily, even minute-by-minute basis —
without having sex. Becoming aware of our inner sense and
experiencing our essence can be as emotionally gratifying as
having sex.

Those of us who have had a desire to leave quickly, or
to say to ourselves, "What was I doing?" after a sexual
encounter, have a heavy armor of ego. If we feel that the
activity has served to tarnish our ego in some way, we will
not feel a closeness and bonding. We are not in tune with
our inner sense and are not living with personal integrity.

An overdeveloped ego keeps us afraid of experiencing
bad relationships. Subsequently, this fear keeps us from
participating fully in relationships. Overcoming fear is a
prerequisite for a healthy, intimate relationship. The ego-
based person finds imperfections with each potential mate;
no one is good enough. But when we say, "No one is good
enough," we are really feeling that way about ourselves.
By looking in the mirror we can see the quality of our closest relationship. If we don't like ourselves, we can't experience the essence of a healthy, loving relationship with
others. We won't believe that we are worthy of receiving
love. Many of us who exercise our sexual preferences
are victims of emotional trauma that lead to our sexual orientation. Unfortunately, it is sometimes easier to explain
gay and uncommon sexual behavior with biology and

genetics than it is to confront the emotional wounds that need healing. Yet we still use sex to test the waters and to feel validated. We want to believe people really do find us attractive and lovable.

When we use sex to satisfy our ego, sex is significantly less satisfying because we are emotionally limited. If we are not emotionally involved, we cannot feel true love. Many people still believe that emotional satisfaction comes primarily from our attractiveness, popularity, and fortune; without this validation from others we must not be acceptable. The assumption is that if we don't have a (sexual) partner or mate, it is because we are not likable or worthy of someone else's love. This explains why society views masturbation as taboo. The logic assumes that if we must engage in self-gratification, we are receiving only physical gratification, not emotional. Sex does not lead to emotional gratification unless it is an expression of love. Lust, on the other hand, often leaves us feeling rejected or empty.

The feeling of alienation is the source of loneliness for many sexual addicts who want to be validated, nurtured, and loved. It is emotional emptiness that keeps voyeurism and pornography as a menace in our society. Despite the ineffectiveness of pornography to fill our emotional voids, many people still don't realize the source of their addiction. Unfortunately, this causes many of us to become the victims of others who use sex to prove their worthiness or express their frustration. The perpetrators are really dissociating from their emotional loneliness and pain by turning to sex. Instead of using masturbation to dissociate from loneliness, severe sexual addicts use others to validate their acceptance. Therefore, we must learn to distinguish those who have an addiction to sex from those whose interest is in establishing a healthy, loving relationship with us. This can be challenging since we are often not aware of our own motives.

People often use sex as a way to feel in control, to feel a sense of power, and to conquer a partner. Due to emotional immaturity, this type of behavior is the demented approach used to feel validated. Sometimes people express underlying anger and frustration through sexual acts.

Women and men (no matter their sexual orientation) use sex as a way to find emotional validation in very much the same way. The outwardly different methods used to attract a partner mask the common motivation between the sexes. While women generally do not use physical strength to control a man, many women will use sexuality to manipulate a partner. This is why we believe men and women view sex differently. Socialization greatly influences gender behavior, but the underlying similarity between men and women is the need for acceptance and harmony.

Ego, Love, and Sex

Love, like energy, never ceases to exist,
it merely waits to reveal itself to those
who are ready to live true to their inner sense.

When discussing sex, often the first question that comes to mind is, "Does this mean love?" As we grow from childhood to adolescence, we increasingly confront our sexuality. During childhood we become aware of the pleasures associated with physical stimulation. Unfortunately, if we were violated sexually as children, we may not remember sex as pleasurable. Still, we attempt to use sex unsuccessfully to regain and validate our self-worth.

We become more aware of the broader consequences of sexual activity when we reach adolescence. Our sexual curiosity is coupled with our strong, ego-based need to feel validated. We seek out partners who find us acceptable but who do not tarnish our image of ourselves. Our sexual encounters are often a reflection of how we feel about ourselves. We sometimes confuse sex with love. We are fooled into believing that passionate sex is an indication of a healthy relationship.

When we allow ourselves to be vulnerable during sex, it feels like love to us. We reveal our true inner sense, if only for a few minutes or seconds. Love is much more than sex and orgasms. Love has little to do with another person. Being in love is about accepting and nurturing ourselves. If we are living true to our inner sense, we will know true love. We will know the essence of where, what, and who we want to be. Love enables us to share generously with others who enter our lives. Our level of self-acceptance determines our capacity to experience love. If you think you have ever been in love and lost, you probably were not in love. Love is more than a feeling; it is a state of mind.

Sex, when used to fulfill the ego, leaves us empty, guilty, lonely, and demoralized. On the other hand, when we use sex to express our emotions of inner peace, it serves as a form of communication. Sex becomes another language for us to express how we are feeling toward ourselves and our partner. Sex is not love but a way for us to express our emotions. If we are feeling anger and frustration, sex takes on an aggressive character. If we are feeling apathetic, sex is just an empty physical activity. If we are feeling content with our ego, sex can be fun. Not until we recognize ourselves as loving people will we experience the joy that we want from our relationships.

Chapter 8

≡ Is the Doctor In?

Improving Health

*Health is recognizing the power of healing
that is present in our inner sense.*

In modern society we have become mentally dependent
on "medicine" to cure our ailments. Modern medicine is
a business, heavily motivated by the need to make a profit.
We believe that we must use the external chemicals we call
drugs to save us; America is a "pill popping" culture. We
are constantly taking this and that pill or syrup for every
minor discomfort. (Even my veterinarian wants to give my
pets drugs when I bring them in for just an overnight board-
ing.) We do not view discomfort as a sign that perhaps our

lives are out of balance and that we need to slow down. Instead, we want the quick "fix" so that we can continue to bury our emotional hurt in our daily activities. Every time we settle for a quick fix we miss the opportunity to reacquaint ourselves with our inner sense, and we forget to stay mentally or spiritually in touch with our bodies.

We seldom give our bodies a chance to generate our own drugs. Also, we often do not consider the use of natural drugs. Natural drugs are those that come from the earth, instead of having an elaborate laboratory create something synthetic. More importantly, we don't believe we have the power to heal. We lack trust in our being.

However, the formula is simple. We need to expand the realm of possibility. Our inner sense will decide what our bodies need. Our inner sense will tell us the following: how much exercise we need, what to eat and how much, how much rest our bodies need, and how much mental stimulation it needs and when. We must simply listen to what our bodies tell us. Have you noticed that when people get sick, the first place they turn for healing is from a doctor, a pharmacist, or even God? We resist acknowledging our own inner powers. Consider how the healing process works when we cut ourselves. We don't heal from the outside but from the inside. A scab covers the wound initially and acts as a natural bandage. Underneath the scab our bodies create healing miracles. When the scab is gone, we can watch the final episode of the healing process as the cut mysteriously disappears. This provides good evidence that if we become inwardly focused we can find the secrets of our own healing.

Parents who are unaware of their inner sense have little chance to educate their children on the connection between spiritual and physical health. This is one of the reasons many of us are not familiar with this idea of personal healing through inner sense. We do not learn to be ultimately responsible for our mental and physical health. Instead, we are very reactionary to health issues.

We often see examples of parents who have good intentions, but who establish unhealthy dietary patterns for their children. There are many advertising campaigns targeted at children and their parents that give the impression big business cares about children. They present us with products, however, that are unsafe to eat and dangerous to play with. Cartoon characters, free gifts, and on-site playgrounds entice unsuspecting customers at restaurants, day-care centers, and schools. These disguises distract us from the essence of what we are really paying for — fat, cholesterol, salt, and sugar, the substances in our diet that have us driving to the local convenience store to buy pills, antacids, and painkillers. These chemicals and the foods we eat cause our bodies to react with tooth decay, poor circulation, high blood pressure, stomach pain, and obesity, to name a few.

Of course, when our bodies are in a state of ill health, we seek more remedies. Off we go to the doctor, who in turn prescribes more medicine. Only this time we can't buy it over the counter, and so we go to the pharmacist and buy the more expensive drugs. By the time we reach adult age, we are often addicted to unhealthy foods, over-the-counter drugs, prescribed drugs, and even illegal drugs. But it's worse than that; we have lost touch with our inner sense, the natural healer!

We invest so much in our ego that we resist the thought of dying before we reach 100 years of age. But despite our attempts to protect ourselves against aging and early death, our fears get the best of us. We believe we need insurance (more big business) to protect us from an unhealthy, dangerous environment full of germs that may kill us prematurely. After we purchase our life insurance policies, we try to slow down our aging process with products to cover our skin and hair so no one knows that we are normal aging humans. We try to convince ourselves that we can defy the energy transformation process. Why do we try to avoid aging? Only our ego knows the answer, and it's not listening to our inner sense. Life is not about longevity; it is about living in harmony with our inner sense. Nothing has ever overcome the natural transformation process we call aging, not even time itself.

The best way to stay healthy is to be healthy. There is no better medicine than knowing that the mind and the body serve one another. The definition of health extends further than cardiovascular capacity or muscle strength. Being aware of our inner sense allows the body and the mind to become one. When our mind and body are in harmony we neutralize toxic chemicals that would otherwise inhabit our bodies. This harmonious state increases our immunity to emotional depression and bodily diseases.

To know when we are suffering from physical or mental ailments, we need to be more aware of our state of being. The body knows how to heal itself, but we can impede the healing process by not listening to our inner sense. We can help in the healing of our bodies by mentally providing it with the proper balance of chemicals. The body generates chemicals naturally and exercise increases the blood flow through the brain and simultaneously distributes the chemicals manufactured by the body. The chemicals generated during exercise help the body to build its immune system. Energy from the brain signals the body to release chemicals that will aid in our healing. The brain acts as a large data base that stores and processes all the information required to have the body function.

The chemical balance in our bodies can be altered by the foods we eat. It is important to pay attention to how our bodies react to different types and quantities of food. Our chemical balance also can change through mental stimulation. If we are excited, our bodies will generate adrenalin. Chemicals flow through our bodies and interact with blood, which carries oxygen and nutrients. Bacteria travel through the body as well and can live in harmony with our bodies unless the chemical balance becomes disturbed. Similarly, in a swimming pool we must continually add chemicals in the right proportions to maintain the proper balance to ward off unwanted bacterial growth. The human body produces and uses its own chemicals. We are our own pharmacists.

When brain energy (chemical and electrical) is in harmony with the universe, we can transmit and receive information or energy to aid in health and healing. There are several areas of brain energy. The most familiar to us is our memory. Unfortunately, memory does not play a very important part in the healing process. Projection or futuring is also a form of brain energy but has little impact on healing since our future is tied to our past. Another area of brain energy deals with the present moment. It is in the present moment that healing takes place. It is also in the present moment that we can realize our essence. Essence defines how we want to experience life in the present moment. Therefore, if our focus is on our essence and on fulfilling our purpose in life, we can find a great source of healing. Fulfilling our purpose does not imply that we must spring from bed and start doing things. When we are not feeling well, we can stay within our essence by accepting our condition without judgment, fear, or resistance. The reason we get sick is so that we can learn how to be healthy. We must let go of our fear of feeling bad and have the patience to watch the transformation of healing.

This does not suggest that modern medicine should be avoided. Some drugs and treatments are quite useful in preventing or controlling disease but often do not help us heal permanently (drugs can even weaken our immune system). However, at issue is the codependency with drugs that is based on fear, the notion that if we don't take the drug we will feel bad. We need to reconsider our reliance on modern medicine and seek to balance our health with the natural healing powers of our immune system.

The power of healing is not in the bandage.

Health is as much about exercising our mental healing abilities as it is about exercising our physical body. Indeed, many of us are still prone to illness or discontent even though we exercise. The reason for this is that most of us are not exercising entirely for health reasons. Instead we allow our ego to motivate us. Exercising for our ego minimizes the benefits to our total health and can even lead to personal training injuries.

Total health is a result of not only exercising our physical bodies but also our internal healing abilities. The mind is healthy when there is a state of harmony between the ego and the inner sense. Therefore, we need to learn to exercise our minds, spirit, and bodies. We must care enough about ourselves to stay in a healthy state of being. This means trying a preventive-maintenance approach to life.

One method of preventing illness comes from a balance of both exercise and relaxation. For those of us who have a hard time relaxing, we must consider relaxation as a form of exercise. Physical exercise, when not motivated by our ego, is a good method for maintaining health because it strengthens the body in several ways: It builds muscle tissue and increases blood flow through the arteries. The increased circulation of blood creates energy, like the generator in a car. As long as we drive the car, the battery recharges. If we let the car sit for too long, the battery dies. Relaxation techniques like meditation can also be helpful as mental or spiritual exercises. We can use these methods to gain greater awareness of the whole mind-body connection. Perhaps if we become aware of our internal body system, we will also find greater spiritual enlightenment.

Good health is not only an individual issue. When we are healthy we also gain the power to heal other forms of life. When we send healing energy outside ourselves (transference), we also become healthier. In the nonphysical world, our brain also can share knowledge from other intelligent energy sources through parallel processing, the ability to deal in the physical and spiritual worlds simultaneously without a shift in consciousness. Our inner sense understands the transference process and gives us the ability to parallel process. For example, we know when energy from other energy sources (sun, water, food, natural chemicals, nurturing energy from humans or animals) can assist in our healing. Transference provides us with an extension of our being and enhances our present moment experience. We can leverage a greater source of healing by sharing energy with nature.

KEYS TO PERSONAL HEALING

(1) Let go of your ego and fear. This releases any stress from the thought of rejection, abandonment, pain, or death. It helps you not to feel guilt or shame.

(2) Know what you want from your life, for it is important to know your essence.

(3) Be still and listen to your mind and body. This will help you be in harmony with nature.

(4) Accept your pain and illness and surrender to it as an acknowledgment of your trust.

(5) Be patient and allow your body and mind the time it needs to heal. You are in a state of transformation.

(6) Give your body the nutrients it needs to boost your immune system. Your body will tell you what types of foods it needs or doesn't want.

(7) Recharge your battery by acting as a generator. Mental and physical exercise are very important to your healing. However, do not exercise on behalf of your ego or pride.

Diets That Restrict Our Flow

*Food cannot fill
the hunger of emotional emptiness.*

The ecosystem is a food chain that sustains the existence of energy in many forms. Food is the basis for our health and is the natural medicine that western cultures have mostly forgotten. Through human ingenuity we have devised ways to provide for ourselves. Technological advances have increased our growing capacity and have increased the longevity of our food supplies. As with most aspects of life, the benefits from advancements in food production are offset by harmful effects on human emotional and physical well-being. For example, we ingest chemicals left as residue from pesticides or chemicals from preservatives, with possible negative side effects that cause cancer or other chemical imbalances in our bodies.

While modern methods of food production have helped to feed many people, they have also led to gluttony in those cultures that have excess food. In many western cultures there is an overconsumption of food. While this generalization may carry some exception, it raises an interesting point: If food is an abundant resource (to the point of waste) in some countries, why should anyone ever go hungry? Technology is available to help manage the distribution issues. Perhaps feeding the hungry is not an issue of capability, but instead an issue of ego intervention by people who thrive on power and control. Much of the starvation in the world could be prevented if the egos of politicians and military people were not at stake. Their lack of compassion and love is really the issue. It follows that setting aside the ego can make a difference in how we influence the world.

In a society where food is available, we still struggle to determine the optimum intake of food required to sustain a mentally and physically healthy life. From birth, many parents or caretakers program us to eat for the taste, not just for sustenance. Another reason we have forgotten how to eat sensibly is because, for many of us, the effort associated with generating food is no longer an issue. If we had to go out for days to hunt food, we would not develop the same eating patterns that are typical in a fast-food lifestyle. Eating would be more focused on rationing, eating essentials, and leaving off the frills of flavor. The foods we now consume are intended to appeal to our tastes. Salt and sugar additives flavor almost everything that is not in its original or natural form. These disguised yet tasteful elements of our diets have us going back for second helpings. Our appetites are prisoners of the "all you can eat" mentality. We often eat until we are uncomfortable. (Children in some western cultures are sometime programmed to eat everything on their plates or have second portions even if they are not hungry.) But digesting large quantities of food is difficult for our bodies. (If we put too much food in our mouths, it is not only very difficult to chew, but hard for our intestines to handle.) Our bodies respond best to a regular feeding schedule with moderate amounts of food. Regularity helps to stabilize our metabolism and keeps us from binging when we get too hungry.

Eating has become a recreational pastime. And like most pleasurable activities, eating has the potential to go beyond sustenance and become addictive. As mentioned earlier, addictions are a way for us to mask our emotional discomfort. If we are overweight we might be using food as an emotional cover-up (we also sometimes use make-up, clothes, body building, hairdos with bangs, and facial hair) to protect ourselves from the outside world. Through our subconscious, food can be used to help us gain weight and to keep people at an emotional distance. Some of us are underweight because we are not comfortable satisfying ourselves. We undereat or binge and purge because we don't believe we deserve to be happy. In our minds we believe if we are thin, people will accept us (at least in some cultures). So instead of keeping people at a distance, underweight people are asking for love and acceptance by not creating distance. In either case, food is used subconsciously to satisfy our emotional emptiness.

Many of us are in a state of perpetual crisis because of the mixed messages we give ourselves. On one hand we seek security and comfort from food, but on the other hand we tell ourselves food is our enemy. We constantly feel guilty for betraying ourselves and "sleeping with the enemy." So how do we overcome this love affair we have with our edible opponent? The obvious answer is to make food an ally. When food becomes our friend we enjoy eating more and, therefore, eat sensibly because we don't have to try and conquer the enemy. The analogy of having a battle with food is a good one because it represents the internal struggle we feel between our ego and inner sense.

If we are dieting for any reason other than our health, we are trying to satisfy our ego. By not comparing ourselves to others or setting goals and time frames to measure our success, we avoid creating emotional obstacles in our lives. If we are trying to measure ego-related results, like the number of pounds lost/gained or the amount of time it takes to lose/gain a pound, we will be distracted from our essence. At this point we have already lost the game. Ego becomes a double-edged sword when it comes to dieting and losing/gaining weight. The good news about ego is that it motivates us to diet. Now for the bad news! If we don't stick to our diets, we feel guilty. Our ego tells us we must be thinner so other people will like us (acceptance is our true motivation for dieting). Only our inner sense knows if our body type is inherently thin, medium, or heavy. Our inner sense knows how to maintain our health and therefore knows when we are overweight or underweight. We don't need to measure our weight on a scale. A diet is nothing more than a description of the food we eat and does not have to be a game we win or lose.

Most diets are not effective because fear is the motivation for dieting. For example, our anxiety may lead us to indulge for several minutes in a snack or meal that tastes great (then we feel bad for the next several hours). It hardly sounds reasonable to spend a very small fraction of time indulging and then spend the larger portion of time regretting our actions. This is a true form of self-punishment. This helps to lower our self-esteem because we tell ourselves we are "bad." To prove how bad we are we find a friend or stranger to whom we can confess our diet sins. Next, we say, "What the hell, this is too much work," and we start eating like we did before. If we don't diet and become thin, we believe people won't like us, and we will suffer social rejection and loneliness. But fear is a self-fulfilling prophecy, so even if we are on a diet we still carry our fears of failure, change, deprivation, and rejection.

We must change our state of mind and learn to accept ourselves as we are. We will lose weight when we stop thinking of ourselves as overweight and start being the person we want to be. We need to remember it is our state of being that causes us to overeat or eat unhealthfully. If we want to lose weight permanently, or maintain our natural weight, our ego state of being cannot stay the same. In other words, let's stop "doing" things differently (eating) and start "being" different. In the end, if we become different, we will make different choices about what we eat. Does this sound too simple? Well, it is!

Inner sense will tell us what we need to know about our diets: when to eat, what to eat, the quantity to eat, the preferred food combinations, and the speed at which to eat. We have the choice to listen to our bodies to determine what we really need. This will help our bodies to stabilize our metabolism. By not focusing on food, our brains stop sending electrical and chemical signals to our body, and our bodies in turn don't react by shedding, retaining, or putting on weight. Once we stabilize our eating patterns and metabolism, our bodies will be whatever we decide we want them to be as long as we are not ego driven.

Knowing the essence of what we really want in life will help us to achieve a healthier state of being. When we make a commitment to our well-being, our diets will automatically change. We can eliminate dieting as a form of punishment and turn eating into a celebration. We don't need to buy special meals, books, memberships to clinics, or other hyped-up schemes designed to reap profits from our insecurities and fears. We can let go of our ego and love ourselves enough to paint the picture of life the way we want to see it.

Fun exercises for playing with food:

Many of us have never tasted the true flavor of vegetables. We believe anything that is not sweet or salty must require some flavor additive. Our salt and sugar addictions provide the evidence. We like butter on our bread because we enjoy the flavor but also because we enjoy the salty taste of the butter. Bread has a wonderful flavor without butter, and salads take on a new character when eaten without dressings; we discover unique flavors that we never knew existed. Meanwhile, our eating disorders keep us from distinguishing between feeling truly hungry or feeling bored and depressed.

Slowing down our chewing can enhance the flavor of food. This gives us the chance to concentrate on each bite or morsel that we place in our mouth. As an experiment, during your next meal start by placing a fingertip-size bite in your mouth. Select one type of unseasoned food. Patiently chew this amount of food and describe the flavor by writing it down or telling someone. Wait before you take the next bite and do the same thing. If you continue this habit, you will find that you eat an appropriate amount and enjoy the gift of food more. Food can also take on a slightly enhanced taste when eaten with the fingers instead of a metal or plastic utensil. As you learn to eat for the essence of sustaining life, you will find that you come closer to your inner sense by eating foods that are closest to their natural state and not combined.

Food combinations can affect how we feel. Most people in the world do not have the luxury of combining so many types of food at one meal. Our digestive system can work most efficiently if we only consume one type of food at a time. Extracting the nutrients from the food we eat is easiest when our bodies are processing only one type of food. Combining certain foods can cause the creation of gas, acids, and chemicals that ultimately affect our energy level and mental alertness, which are critical to our health. Consider eating citrus fruit, nuts, beans, grains, and vegetables separately. Meat is not essential to a meal unless there is no other source of food available.

TIPS ON EATING OUT:

(1) EAT OUT AT HOME

Preparing your own food can be fun and can ensure that food is cooked to your taste. Eating at home not only helps you to consume food prepared the way you want it but also saves money.

(2) USE A DOGGIE BAG

This is a good way to avoid eating the food combinations and large quantities served at many restaurants. It also reduces food waste.

(3) ORDER FROM THE KITCHEN

Many restaurants will prepare a special meal for you that isn't on the menu. Tell your waiter what you want and how it should be prepared. This is sometimes cheaper than the menu items.

(4) SELECT NATURAL FOOD RESTAURANTS

Many towns and cities now have at least one or two vegetarian or natural food restaurants. They are sometimes located in or affiliated with a natural foods grocery. Usually, these types of restaurants offer meals made from organically grown products.

(5) STAY FOCUSED ON THE ESSENCE OF WHAT YOU WANT

Remember that you are eating primarily for sustenance.

Part Three

Defining Your Essence

❖   ❖   ❖

Chapter 9

What Is Essence?

Defining Your Essence

*You can't find what you are looking
for in life, you can only live it.*

Life exposes us to so many choices, yet the demands to
conform to the latest trends are overwhelming. What
is the right direction for us? Often we allow the decision to
be made for us. We accept ideas, fads, and suggestions
without considering if they fit our personal style or lead us
where we want go. Many of us have forgotten how to take
responsibility for our lives. We have been programmed by
family, peers, schools, organizations, churches, and the
media. We relinquish our freedom because we do not know

what we want from life. If we do know, we are afraid to ask for what we want, so we settle for what we get. We then compare and measure ourselves against others to decide how successful we are. Too often, our evaluation makes us feel mediocre or inadequate and our ego sets destructive emotions into action; we feel angry, cheated, violated, demoralized, shamed, or guilty. Our behavior becomes a reaction to our emotions. We either surrender our lives to our emotions, in which case we act out our anger, or we avoid our emotions by denying that they exist. This is precisely how we end up in crisis.

Many of us believe we should be happy with the hand we have been dealt, while others feel that they have been dealt an unfair hand. Until we know our purpose in life, we will not take advantage of the cards we have. We will play our cards in a way that leaves us emptyhanded and emotionally broke. When our lives come upon crisis, only then do we begin to evaluate the cards, consider shuffling the deck, and decide to play, using a different strategy or a different game with different rules. We often ignore our mind's ability to see and create other possibilities. We lose our imagination, our creativity of thought. We don't understand our purpose. Maybe we don't need to play at all; perhaps we were meant to be dealers instead.

Because of our ego, we typically evaluate life from an external perspective. Life need not be evaluated in terms of success or failure. Instead, we can assess our purpose and level of fulfillment. Life's experiences determine our level of fulfillment, not what we can show for it. Besides our personal definition of success, the bottom line is not money but how we feel about ourselves. Since financial wealth or material acquisitions don't guarantee happiness, the only place we can expect to find happiness is from being in our essence. Essence is not usually a part of our conscious thoughts when we operate from our ego. We become so focused on what we don't want that we forget what it is we really do want. We spend too much time complaining instead of creating what we want. We interject words like *never, always, better,* and *more* in our sentences, not realizing that these words propel us to the past or future and keep us from staying present in the moment. It takes time to bring an awareness of our essence to a point of consciousness.

The first clue to understanding the essence of life is to remember that essence cannot be described in tangible or measurable form (time, money, weight, inches, or material objects). Any object or activity that can be experienced in a tangible way defines its physical form. Our inner sense knows the essence of life. To experience our essence we need to understand our true emotional desires; then we can focus on the life experience we would like to have.

The second clue to discovering our essence is to avoid any attempt to satisfy our ego or anything designed to make us more acceptable in the eyes of others. By ignoring our ego needs, we also avoid the fears that prohibit us from living true to our essence. For example, if we decide to lose weight and improve our physical condition by getting in shape, we must first be aware of the "essence" of what we really want. The essence of what we really want is self-respect and self-acceptance. Getting in shape to improve our health is living true to essence because becoming healthier is an act of self-respect and vice versa.

Essence, like fear, is a self-fulfilling prophecy. We must allow our inner sense to replace our ego in order for us to recognize the essence of what we want. Once we program our lives with our essence, our inner sense converts to autopilot mode. If our fears (ego) cause us to take over the controls, we get off course and risk danger. For most of us who are not familiar with the sophistication of modern avionics, trusting an autopilot may require a leap of faith. However, trusting our internal autopilot function (inner sense) is essential to helping us steer safely through the uncertainty of life's circumstances brought on by our ego.

Remember, we are closest to our essence when we stop evaluating and judging our self-worth and our material worth. If we want to be independent from our jobs or our debts, then a sense of freedom is the essence of what we want, and money is the form. Our inner sense will start to provide for our freedom if we stay focused on the essence of feeling free and not on earning money. However, if we want money to satisfy our ego, we may become wealthy, but we may still feel trapped and never achieve personal freedom.

Over time, an awareness of our essence becomes a subconscious component of our being, and we live fluently from our inner sense. Without this level of consciousness that stems from our inner sense, prayer or meditation is somewhat ineffective in helping us to experience our essence. Too often, we use prayer to change someone or something for our own benefit. When we finally realize that the only thing we can change is the thoughts we have about how we live our own lives, then we will see miracles happen. This is the ultimate state of Enlightenment, Nirvana, or Heaven. Unfortunately, some religions have taught us that this state of euphoria is not attainable if we are alive. Surprise! It is possible! However, we must not confuse our feelings of momentary happiness derived from an ego event with the beauty of a permanent state of inner peace.

This section will help you discover your essence. You will learn what is truly important to you. You will decide what values bring you the greatest fulfillment. This information will not tell you what to do. You don't have to do anything! But awareness is essential. You will need to decide if your thoughts and actions are consistent with your essence. Ask yourself this question, "Is my current state of being allowing me to experience the essence of what I want?" The answer is simply "Yes" or "No." Your actions either align to the desires of your ego or to your inner sense.

The site of it maid it rong
even tho it sownded rite, thairfor,
he who understands the essence of life
has no concern about the form.

On page 116 is a chart that can be used to define key elements of our lives. There are three internal and three external factors. By combining these elements together in a matrix format, we can identify our essence. This chart can help us visualize how our internal state of being relates to those external areas of our lives that are important to a high level of fulfillment. When we integrate both the internal factors with the external factors, we create a matrix consisting of nine boxes.

The nine boxes in the matrix are like a palette from which we can paint a picture of our lives. Each box represents a different color on the palette. As artists we can blend the colors in our lives. If we define the essence of our lives using these boxes, our actions become like the stroke of a brush. We can learn to paint a picture of our Heaven on earth. With every moment that passes, life provides us with an empty canvas. Through personal development and awareness we blend colors from our palette and enhance the beauty of our lives. Together our thoughts and the delicate stroke of our actions can create a masterpiece.

Below are the definitions of the key elements that help us determine our essence:

EXTERNAL FACTORS

These are the primary areas of our lives that receive most of our attention as humans. We invest in our relationships, environment, and our chosen profession, hoping to find happiness and fulfillment.

Relationships

We do not need to make any distinctions between family, friends, co-workers, romantic partners, strangers, animals, or plants. To experience our essence we strive to create quality relationships with all living things.

Environment

The environment relates to where we are physically or mentally, the location where we choose to live, or maybe a place we dream about. Some people prefer big cities, small towns, mountains, beaches, deserts, cold climates, or tropical climates. We select these types of environments because they are where we can best fulfill our purpose.

Profession

A profession is what we choose as a preferred method of providing for our sustenance or our basic survival needs. While a profession may be a job, it does not necessarily have to be viewed as work or a career; we are entitled to enjoy other aspects of our chosen profession other than just money or title. We need to know how we can best contribute to ourselves and others in intangible ways. This is the essence of our chosen profession.

INTERNAL FACTORS

How we experience happiness and fulfillment is determined by our thoughts, our emotions, and our health. In these areas of our existence we create our reality. We can either be consumed by fear, or we can focus on what we really want.

Thoughts

We think continuously. We often aren't aware of our thoughts. Our thoughts usually evoke some level of emotion. Therefore, it is important to be aware of what we think about. We can figure out our essence by thinking about what we really want from our external world in the form of intangible rewards.

Emotions

Since emotions result from our thoughts, it is important that our thoughts reflect the type of emotions we want to feel. When we exclude the ego and monetary or material wealth from our list of desires, we have the essence of what we truly want to feel.

Health

Our life experiences are more rewarding when we maintain our health. Health includes both our physical and mental well-being. We must understand how our external environment affects our health. When we nurture ourselves, we are more aware of what jeopardizes our health. We experience essence when we respect ourselves enough to protect our health.

The first chart on page 112 gives examples of ego-based desires. These are the typical things we believe are important. However, this chart uses material and ego-oriented descriptions and would not represent the essence of our desires. The second chart gives examples of how we can describe the essence of what we want without describing it in form.

INSTRUCTIONS FOR DEFINING YOUR ESSENCE:

As you use the matrix on page 116 to define your essence, avoid describing your essence with ego-based adjectives like appreciated, acknowledged, rewarded, and accepted. Take time to think about what you want. This is your chance to ask for everything you want, so be sure to exhaust all the possibilities that describe what you want. Select only the words that have special meaning to you. If the words used at the bottom of page 112 also reflect your essence, then include them. Fill all nine boxes with words that describe what you want in that aspect of your life.

Make sure you follow the guidelines described below. Remember, your thoughts are what you think about what you want. Your emotions are the feelings you want to experience because of your thoughts. Health is the combination of thoughts and emotions that support your physical and mental well-being. You may use the same feelings repeatedly in any box.

Guidelines:

1) Your Essence does not include anything used to satisfy your ego.

2) Your Essence does not include anything tangible or measurable.

3) Your Essence does not include anything that avoids your fears.

Caution:

You must become personally aware of your motivations for what you want. Always be sure to ask yourself why this thought or feeling is important to you. If it relates to another person or your fear of rejection, abandonment, pain, or death, do not include that word in the boxes.

EXAMPLE OF LIVING FROM YOUR EGO DESIRES

EXTERNAL

	Relationships	Environment	Profession
Thoughts	*smart* *good job* *athletic*	*big house* *good shopping* *entertainment*	*pays well* *good position* *travel*
Emotions	*accepted* *attractive* *sexy*	*safe* *wealthy* *popular*	*recognized* *important* *successful*
Health	*lose weight* *diet*	*health club* *golf course*	*no manual labor*

(left side label: I N T E R N A L)

EXAMPLE OF LIVING FROM YOUR ESSENCE

EXTERNAL

	Relationships	Environment	Profession
Thoughts	*honesty* *trust* *self-acceptance*	*warmth* *peace* *beauty*	*creativity* *helping others* *freedom*
Emotions	*love* *happy* *oneness*	*harmony* *calm* *peaceful*	*energetic* *enthusiastic* *fulfillment*
Health	*loving* *healing* *nurturing*	*clean air* *relaxing* *exercising*	*relaxing* *movement*

(left side label: I N T E R N A L)

*Peace is when you can visualize the trickle
of a mountain stream,
the splashing of an ocean wave,
or dancing leaves in the summer breeze
living inside your body.*

Visualization Exercise:

To help you get started identifying your essence, relax! You may need to close your eyes occasionally to help you visualize. Envision your body as a limp, wet cloth. Your muscles are sagging. Picture a natural setting that is appealing to you. Let that picture come to life through animation. Imagine the wind blowing gently through the leaves, or the stream flowing through the woods on a fall day, or the waves lapping on a secluded beach lined with palm trees. Feel at peace without any worries. You do not have to worry about being lonely because this "special place" is filled with love. This is your "special place." Money is no issue because there is nothing to buy. Everything you need is provided for you. Create your peaceful setting.

Take a deep breath and then exhale. Now imagine that this scene is part of you. It lives inside you. And you can feel the motion of the wind and the warmth of the sun. You can hear the sounds of the water as it flows over the rocks in the creek or crashes on the beach. See the trickling dewdrops glisten like diamonds in the sun. Listen to the birds. Smell the freshness of the crisp morning air and the bouquet of a field of wildflowers. When your image of Heaven comes alive for you, then you will experience your essence. Open your eyes. Keep the feeling you just had. It is yours to carry with you. You can create that place and feeling anytime you like. It is always waiting for you. Simply let go of your ego and surrender to the essence of your inner sense.

Ask yourself why you are not experiencing the essence of your desires. The answer is, most likely, your fear of the unknown. But what do you have to lose? Recall the essence of what you really want. Is your essence not more desirable than what you have been experiencing in life? Ask yourself again, "What is the essence of how I would like my life experience to be?" Feel free to acknowledge the feelings you truly want in life and to behave in ways that reinforce those feelings. Discovering and experiencing your essence is not possible unless you let go of your ego, fear, and pride. This is a major act of courage.

Your essence may seem too good to come true. Maybe you are thinking, "I can't have all that." Fortunately, essence is not something you wait, wish, or hope for, nor is it an expectation of things to come. Essence is a statement of the way you want to experience life, the state of being who you truly are from your inner sense. You can start living the life you want right now. You must trust that everything you want is available to you. To attain your essence you must realize it is not a goal, but your purpose in life. Know and trust that your inner sense will allow you to live true to your essence. Be patient, for it is not until you learn to accept where you are today that you will be allowed to go someplace different tomorrow. As long as you try to change your external environment you will stay exactly where you are. Again, essence like fear is a self-fulfilling prophecy because *as you think so shall your life be*.

The table below illustrates the differences in approach between our ego and our inner sense. Ego tells us what to do and our inner sense shows us how to be. If we follow our ego, we will get what we need (to learn) and not what we want. Inner sense, by contrast, allows us to experience our essence.

EGO	vs.	INNER SENSE	
(What we do) =	*(What we get)* =	*(Our state of being)* =	*(We get the essence of what we want)* =
Seek relationships	Rejection	Be loving to everyone	LOVE
Work	Money	Be joyful	HAPPINESS
Vacation	Escape	Be free	FREEDOM
Control others	Controlled	Be still	PEACE
Protect ourselves	Isolation	Be trusting	TRUST
Manipulate others	Adversaries	Be honest	HONESTY
Take medicine/ diet	Dependence	Be healthy	HEALTH

See the next page for your work sheet.

WORKSHEET FOR DEFINING YOUR ESSENCE

Guidelines:

1) Your Essence does not include anything used to satisfy your ego.

2) Your Essence does not include anything tangible or measurable.

3) Your Essence does not include anything that avoids your fears.

	EXTERNAL		
	Relationships	Environment	Profession
I N T E R N A L Thoughts			
Emotions			
Health			

Meditation

Only after you have found the melodies of
silence will you begin to hear the music of life.

Meditation means different things to different people. There are many techniques that teach us how to meditate. Some people prefer sitting to lying down to reduce the chance of falling asleep. Others use a mantra, which is a word or sound they repeat over and over, silently or aloud. Quiet soothing music is effective for some, while others prefer total silence. Despite the method you choose, meditation is the process of consciously calming your mental and physical body. Since we are constantly having thoughts race through our minds, meditation provides us an opportunity to slow down our thoughts temporarily. Meditation is a form of relaxation; we can use it to remove ourselves from the worries of daily living and reduce our stress level. Meditation is also helpful when we use it to identify our essence and purpose in life. Being within our essence and living with purpose is a true form of enlightenment.

Meditation without purpose and essence is merely like taking a daily tranquilizer. Because of the freeing effects of meditation it has the potential to be used as a drug. Similar to experiencing a drug high, the effects of meditation wear off after time. Therefore, the benefits of meditation become diluted if we become compulsive or addicted to meditation. Under this circumstance, missing one's meditative session only creates more stress and insecurity. In other words, many people who meditate approach meditation as an activity to reduce stress and momentarily dissociate from their ego. There is more to realizing our potential than meditation. In our search for greater fulfillment it is interesting that we may never consider eliminating the source of stress altogether. The reason is we have not realized that meditation can be a permanent state of awareness.

Living true to our essence means we can ultimately eliminate the need to meditate on a routine schedule. Our consciousness assumes a meditative state at all time. While this may seem like an impossibility, it can be done by simply changing our lifestyles, incorporating our essence, and letting go of our ego and stress. As long as our focus is on our essence, it really doesn't matter if we meditate or not because we will be living according to our inner sense. Our lives will inherently become stress free.

The best way for us to connect with spiritual energy is to stay true to our essence, be aware of our inner sense, and to trust that everything we want is in the process of becoming our reality. We don't have to do anything other than just live consciously in every moment. When we are in the present moment, our inner sense will help us to know when we need to relax, connect spiritually with other energy, and to meditate. We do not need a daily regime to stay centered.

Meditation Exercise:

While there are many techniques used to meditate, the one I like the best is discovering the universe through our mind's eye. It's like having a telescope focused on your inner sense. Try the following meditation exercise: Sit or lie in a comfortable position. Silence is not absolutely necessary. You may prefer to play soothing music while you meditate. Close your eyes and examine the back of your eyelids. You will notice different patterns of light and dark. As your eyes move around, the patterns will change. Some will fade and new ones will appear. Enjoy the show! Keep your eyes closed and try to see through your eyelids to a point in the

darkness about three feet in front of you. You will
need to concentrate on that spot. As you do, you
may notice a glowing light. Try to keep your eyes
still and focused on that spot. Concentrate and
notice your breathing as it becomes calm. Next,
with your eyes still closed, roll your eyes up and
focus on the back of your head. Pay attention to
what you see. Focus as deep inside yourself as you
can. Picture the most peaceful and beautiful place
you can. Imagine that place existing inside your
body. Now try to find where this beautiful place
begins and ends. You may notice it blends in with
other scenery in your mind's eye, which is actually
a window to the universe. You can look into your
own soul, body, and beyond to other galaxies in the
universe. This is possible because we are a universe
within a universe, and we share the same energy.

This meditative technique is one exercise that
may allow you to see your inner sense more clearly.
If you cannot relate to this exercise, you may need to
find other ways to explore the world beyond your
conscious, logical mind. When you are looking deep
inside yourself, you can find the answers to questions you have about your life and discover your
other self (inner sense); you can define your essence.

Religion

*He who walks with spiritual dignity
crosses no boundaries.*

A good definition of religion is a set of institutionalized
beliefs. When we practice religion as part of a group,

unconsciously, it allows us to give up our responsibility and accountability to find the truth. However, once we begin living our essence, we notice that most religions operate from the ego of their clergy and members. They control the "followers" or "believers." By teaching its members to conform, organized religion becomes nothing more than the packaging and marketing of a set of beliefs. Many religions run like big business and are highly focused on the monetary contributions required for growth. For a church (organization, cult, association, club, etc.), growth means power, influence, and money. These things are the essence for some organized religions. Many of us stay attached to our churches because they provide a social environment that fulfills the need of our ego. In the church we find security, validation, and a reinforcement of old traditional beliefs that we dare not question with the intelligence of our inner sense. Perhaps this explains why most of us who have a strong faith in God (or anything external to ourselves) don't seem to attain Heaven on earth.

Unfortunately, many religions also become plagued with rituals and traditions that lead to the belief that redemption stems from symbolic actions we must perform. The assumption is that without this action we will not be forgiven or accepted. Many of us who belong to the congregation live in a perpetual state of fear that we are not meeting the basic requirements to ensure our eternity. However, when we enter a state of being that is in harmony with our inner sense, we lose our need to pray or meditate as a form of action because we become one with our creator. Our lives become the meditation and we become our prayers.

What about God? The reason most of us can't find God is the same reason we can't find love. As a popular song once hinted, we're looking in all the wrong places. Where do we find God? It's simple. God is our inner sense. God is universal energy, and God is our individual energy.

Despite our religion, we realize God when our spirit connects with the energy of the universe. The rituals and
traditions we wrap around our beliefs distract us from
experiencing God. We get too invested in selling our religion and allow our egos to lead us astray. For many of us,
it is easy to avoid holding ourselves accountable for our
actions and thoughts when we believe God is external to
ourselves. This is a fundamental point of contention
between religions. Again, we get consumed in the debate
and lose the awareness of our inner sense. There is evidence that we are a manifestation of God; for example, we
possess the power of healing. Think about how the magic
of healing is an inside-to-outside process. Of course, due
to low self-esteem and years of social conditioning, we
deny the power of our inner sense. We tell ourselves, "I'm
not good enough to be God. I'm only human." We are all
God. We are all energy, and we are all miraculous. We
need to acknowledge our true power.

If we discovered our inner sense, we wouldn't use religion to separate ourselves from others. We wouldn't use
religion to be judgmental of others who we feel don't conform to our expectations. God is not found in conformity.
God is not found in our ego. God cannot evaluate us or
judge if we are right or wrong. God exists when we arrive
at a place in our lives where we find balance and harmony
in our being. God is merely a state of being that is available
to each of us who is willing to live true to our inner sense.

People who have experienced near-death recall the
beauty of their experience. They feel euphoric because they
have relinquished their ego and witnessed their true inner
sense. This type of euphoria is available to us without
encountering near-death or death as we know it. The concept of reaching Heaven has been misunderstood because
some religions speak of dying as a prerequisite to entering
Heaven. Christian religion teaches us that when we die
then we can enter the "Kingdom of God" called Heaven.
The words from scripture are often taken literally. I share

another interpretation. The reference to death means to allow our ego and past to die because they influence our future. The death of our ego and our fears gives us the ability to enter, not the gate of, but the state of Heaven. Heaven is just around the corner from our ego, at a place called "inner sense." Therefore, Heaven is not something we have to wait for. God and Heaven are one. We reach a state of Heaven when we live true to our God, or inner sense. Heaven is really the point in our lives when we recognize the core essence of our desires. When we let ego die, we can be reborn and discover our inner sense, or God.

Religion provides hope for many people. Hope is not knowledge or a belief. Hope is a projection of wishful thoughts. We could spend our lives hoping that God will change us and improve our lives, but our lives will change in the direction we want when we discover our essence and follow our inner sense. Hope is the result of interpreting God as external to our being. When we learn to accept our lives exactly as we live them and focus on the essence of what we desire, then our lives will be transformed. Hope is really the desire of people who are not living from their essence in the present moment. When we mentally and spiritually experience our essence, we find that hope has little value. Hope exists only without knowledge. Inner sense is knowledge, and hope becomes an irrelevant thought.

Faith is like hope unless we take personal responsibility for acknowledging our essence and the power of our inner sense. Faith in a set of beliefs that are given to us by someone else provides us with little ownership of our lives; we live from a set of assumptions that we seldom challenge or verify. This type of blind faith is a facade for those who are not willing to let go of their ego or fear. Such faith is common for the conformist, perfectionist, and defeatist. On the other hand, faith when derived from our souls takes on a different characteristic. Not until we experience faith as true knowledge, instead of as a belief, will we see the first miracle in our lives. The faith we have in our inner sense is our spiritual knowledge that works miracles in our lives. Without knowledge we are susceptible to bearing witness to a false God called ego. Only when we are operating in the realm of our essence do we experience the power of our faith. If we spend time praying, hoping, going regularly to church, observing religious dogma, historic rituals, and traditions out of fear, we may never recognize our true essence. Instead we believe that our day in the sun will come by "doing the right things." Now is the opportunity to stop "doing" and to start being true to our essence. We cannot "act" our way to Heaven. If our state of being does not include self-love, sincere compassion, understanding, tolerance, patience, forgiveness, and generosity, we will be assured we will not attain a state of Heaven. We cannot be in a phase of adult theatrics and expect to reap the rewards of faith. Integrity is an integral characteristic of inner peace. It is the difference between Heaven and Hell.

The night before his death, the late Dr. Martin Luther King, Jr., in his famous "Mountain Top" speech, gave a message to the world about living. He talked about the uncertainty of life and about how controlling or predicting the future was not of paramount concern. In this powerful sermon Dr. King beautifully articulated the notion of living beyond one's fear. An extrapolation of his famous words might be that he was talking about conquering the mountain (ego) and looking to the other side (our inner sense). This act of being in essence is in fact glorious and is synonymous with God's will. It is when we are living within the integrity of our essence that we witness or experience the divine, The Promised Land.

Essence

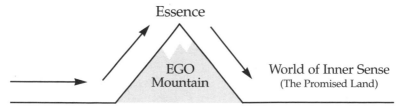

EGO
Mountain

World of Inner Sense
(The Promised Land)

All this raises the issue of the hereafter. You may be thinking, "If I can reach the Promised Land while I'm still living, do I have to give up my right to eternal life?" Stop worrying! Energy never ceases to exist — it merely transforms itself; energy guarantees our eternity. However, if our ego is alive and well, we probably worry more about our impact on this world or our legacy after we die. We can make the largest contribution to humanity by experiencing our essence on earth. If our focus is on essence, we instinctively share energy with all life. There is nothing tangible about our essence. Review the chart you filled in earlier that describes your essence. It is precisely these things you described as your essence that will be transferred to future generations both spiritually and genetically. The contribution you make while living within your essence will be felt for an eternity.

Chapter 10

Getting to the Essence

The Self-Development Process

*The frequency of our
happiness is determined by
the ability to appreciate our memories
in the context of tomorrow.*

Watching our lives is much like watching a fire. At birth, we are placed in this human existence like logs freshly placed on a fire. It takes a lot of energy to get us started. We get our start from another energy source. Once we have been ignited by the embers of other logs, we begin to burn on our own. As we burn, life will occasionally come along and stoke us. We adjust to the change and we begin to burn other dimensions of ourselves. As we continue to burn, we notice signs of age as the outer bark is stripped away and the energy from the fire transforms us. During the constant process of burning, energy is transformed into light and heat. Eventually, we break into smaller pieces of hot embers, no longer generating the large flames we once did, but now providing the source of energy to help start new logs placed on the fire. Finally, we turn to ashes and dust. This is life!

The energy from our ego fuels our lives. Ego keeps us drowning in our dissatisfaction and discomfort. We drown in our worries and problems, and we panic our way through life. Constantly, we react and worry where our next breath of air will come from. In fact, often those who suffer or are less fortunate are closest to their inner sense. After we pass fear and truly confront death, our bodies enter a state of shock or suspended life. At that point we either make the transition through death or we continue to invest in our ego and hang on to life. As mentioned earlier, near-death experiences can be very humbling and magical. When we are in harmony with nature and living from our inner sense, we learn to relax. Our natural buoyancy allows us to float and experience the essence of the life we want to enjoy. Too often, we feel we constantly have to stroke and paddle to keep from drowning in our ego-based world.

In our search to find a more fulfilling existence we locate information, self-help programs, therapists, workshops, or group counseling that help shine light on our lives. These programs are often like walking into a dark room with a flashlight. We discover what is in that one area of our lives where we choose to focus the light, but there are many interesting things in the dark room of life. True discovery comes when we use the flashlight to examine things in the room we haven't yet seen. Our most revealing moments are when we find the light switch and illuminate the whole room. Essence is the light switch to our lives.

When we understand the essence of our desires and start living in harmony with those desires, our whole lives will light up. Once we see the whole room, we realize that our previous perceptions of the room may not have been accurate. From that moment on we have the choice to live differently. We are no longer confined by the darkness. We don't have to fear stumbling over an obstacle we can't see, like bad relationships, jobs we don't like, bad investments, and so on. We have the opportunity for a new life filled with greater confidence and a sense of purpose. Some of us will take the challenge while others will remain in adult theatrics until the next crisis arises.

Most of us prefer life to be predictable. We resist change, even if we are in an unhappy situation. Since we believe the only way to change our lives is to take action and do something, we resist the effort and we fear the possible negative effects that might cause us pain or failure. In our minds, we already know how to deal with our current state of discomfort. If we do anything differently, we will be forced to deal with a new set of circumstances that might cause us more pain that we won't know how to handle. A vicious cycle ensues.

Over time, we learn to perceive life through association of our experiences. By living in external orientation through our ego, we fail to consider that every experience is unique, new, and different from the ones we've had before. We paint our reality, learn how to live within the picture we paint for ourselves, and never realize that we have access to more canvas, different brushes, and different-colored paints. Our ego is greatly responsible for how we perceive life. The ego colors our experiences and interprets them into our reality. All things that exist in our minds are real to us because we can ultimately attach meaning to them when we filter them through our ego. Eventually, perception and reality become one. Every moment that we are alive we carry with us, in memory, our reality as filtered by the ego. We use our logical mind to project into the future. The more we anticipate the future, the more we close our thoughts to the possibility of an outcome that we have not predetermined. Our lives soon become a self-fulfilling prophecy. We are convinced that we are limited to the life we have come to expect. Our physical senses then experience life the way the mind has told us it should be. This explains why when we see, hear, touch, smell, or feel something familiar to us, we either react favorably or distance ourselves.

We live like puppets tied to the strings of our memories. Though we may want a different life circumstance, the strings of the past pull us away from a healthier reality. So we diet, exercise, complain, and break up or hold on to relationships, trying to give ourselves an opportunity for another beginning. Yet our vision of a better life becomes distorted as our vision for the future passes through the prism of our past negative, and sometimes positive, experiences. Despite how much we would like to avoid the uncomfortable aspects of life or would like to hold on to the positive aspects, it is only possible to develop a greater sense of awareness at a rate equal to our experiences. Despite our attempts to deny our attachment to the past, we cannot totally hide from our experiences because they are responsible for who we are today. Those experiences will continue to influence our state of being unless we become more aware of how our attachments to the past are satisfying our ego and creating a volatile sense of reality. Cutting the strings that attach us to ego, fear, and low self-esteem will help to free us from our past.

The next diagram illustrates how our ego acts as a filter to influence our beliefs about how the world relates to us. The ego filters our five physical senses (sight, smell, taste, touch, and sound) and integrates them with our thoughts that, in turn, generate our beliefs about our world. The inner circle of the diagram called awareness is normally disclosed to us after we reach a point of crisis. Awareness is the acknowledgment that things may not be exactly as they appear through our ego filters. Knowledge is the center of our being. Thus, we are the inherent knowledge that comes from our inner or sixth sense.

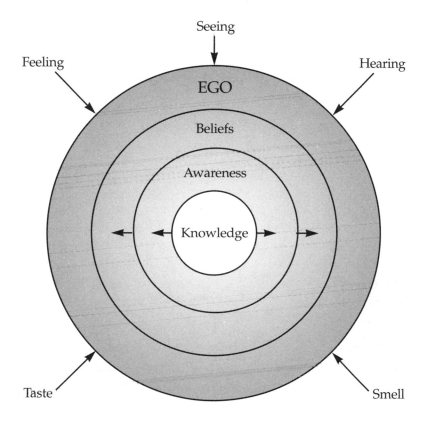

As we discover our inner sense, we realize that we have inherent knowledge available to us. The arrows pointing outward from the center circle in the diagram above show that it is from this inherent knowledge that we can alter how we think, how we believe, and how our five senses experience the world around us. This inherent knowledge is the source of our instincts and intuition. Our inner sense knows everything it needs to. This intelligent energy knows enough to power our immune system, nervous system, brain, cardiovascular flow, and digestive system. Our molecular link to energy in the universe is the source of true knowledge. Through the awareness and development of our mental and physical being, we experience a transformation of our ego-based thoughts. Our thoughts and our physical nervous system ultimately determine how we experience life.

You don't have to work at life.
It will work for you.

Once we overcome our fears, live with trust and love, let go of our ego, stop measuring, judging, and defining our experiences, and learn to think in essence and not in form, we will embark upon an exciting and joyous journey. The essence of our desires is not an end in itself but a journey of joy and purpose.

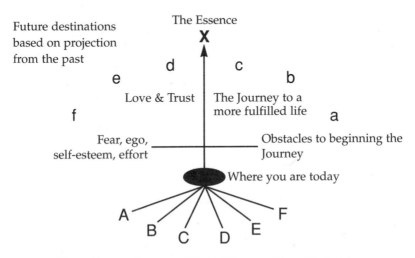

Past Experiences That Shape Our Future

To live life to the fullest
we have to sometime know what we need, not what we want.

The diagram on the previous page gives an illustration of the dynamics involved in creating our reality and living our essence. This personal development model describes how our experiences influence our future reality. The diagram further shows the obstacles that keep us from experiencing our essence. If we are honest, we can use this diagram to identify where we are in our thought process at any point in our lives. Remember, our thoughts and beliefs stem from mixing thoughts from our past with those of the current moment. We then feel good, angry, or perhaps sad, based on how we integrate the past and present together, which then determines how we project the future to be. (Of course, we must realize that the future is just an illusion and never actually arrives.) By living from our inner sense or inner knowledge, we can become less judgmental and more open-minded by staying only in the present moment. When we learn to accept our experiences or the events in our lives without viewing them as permanent, we can stay open to new possibilities for living our essence.

The following explanation of this diagram may help make this phenomena more clear: At the bottom of the diagram are the upper case letters "A" through "F." These letters represent any number of experiences we have had in our lives. These experiences happened to us when we were living from our ego. Therefore, these experiences were only real from the perspective of our ego; they shaped our perception of reality. These are the experiences that stay attached to us like strings to a puppet, causing us to react constantly to life.

The circle represents where we are today. If we continue to live our lives heavily influenced by our ego, we will predetermine our future even before it happens. This, of course, creates anxiety and stress as we anticipate reliving the past again. The influence of our past (A-F) on our future is represented by the corresponding lower case characters "a" through "f." Without realizing it, we react to situations and events based on old information. If we want to experience a more fulfilling present or future, then we want to avoid thinking about the past as if it were the present or future. We need to detach the strings (A-F) that keep us connected to our past. Yes, it means letting go of our past perceptions and experiences. Every experience from this point forward can be explored with innocence (inner sense). Forget what you used to believe to be true — it may not be true anymore! (My intuitive knowledge tells me that more than fifty percent of what we learned about life in the past is no longer applicable.)

Our biggest obstacle to a more fulfilled life is represented by the horizontal line just above the circle. This line represents the barrier created by our fear of trusting our inner sense, letting go of our past, relinquishing control, and expending effort. It also represents our ego's need for preservation and acceptance due to our lack of self-confidence, and the belief we are not worthy of a more rewarding life. It further represents how we keep ourselves locked in ignorance about what is possible for us. This line shows how our past takes control of our lives repeatedly by creating a false truth for us. It represents an illusion of the effort required to enjoy the essence of what we want.

The path to realizing our essence is through recognizing the possibilities that exist when we trust our inner sense. We will experience the essence (X on the diagram) of our desires. It is our responsibility to ensure that our desires are in harmony with nature. Since physical form is in a constant state of transformation, we won't find happiness if we are stuck on the importance of the physical world. Therefore, if we try to keep energy in a fixed state, we create disappointment. A static existence is contrary to the natural flow of energy and causes us to be out of harmony.

We must be willing to accept change and a new reality. Everything we want is already available and is in the process of happening as we let go of our ego. Watch as a new life unfolds with the splendor of a miracle!

Exercise to rewrite your life's script:

An effective technique for safely remembering the dramatic events that we are attached to recognizes that we cannot change the events in our lives, but that perhaps we can change the memory of them. Since memories are merely energy in the form of thoughts, we can change our memory by changing our thoughts. This sounds easy; however, it seems difficult because we resist changing our thoughts. We are attached to our thought processes because they are familiar to us, and we believe that they are the best way for us to survive. Unfortunately, our current memories or thoughts may lead to beliefs that prevent us from experiencing a more satisfying life and leave us with a negative self-image. This may be why some theorists believe we only use three to five percent of our brain's capacity. We avoid exploring how we might access the other ninety-five percent when our subconscious and conscious thoughts are filtered through the prism of our experiences and the associated memories.

Our memory of the events that happened to us is not necessarily a one-hundred-percent accurate accounting of what actually transpired. Even though terrible things do happen to us, sometimes our responses make the memories far more traumatic than the event itself. We create the drama because it helps justify our emotions at the time. We often either repress these events and the feelings surrounding them, or we might exaggerate the memories. By exaggerating an event, we can receive greater attention from others as we communicate our tragedies (ego boost). If we repress or deny the memories, we also deny our feelings and may emotionally shut down. Unfortunately, as we convince ourselves that our lives were not and are not filled with love, security, and acceptance, we also convince ourselves we are not worthy of these things. We stay stuck for many years because our subconscious has been programmed with these thoughts, and despite our attempts to consciously change our lives, our subconscious sabotages our good intentions.

So how do we reorient our subconscious minds so that we experience what we want? As simple as it may seem, it is similar to changing the program in a computer. You take out the old one and install the new program: by recreating our memories the way we would prefer to respond to them, by taking responsibility for being inwardly versus externally oriented, and by always creating what we want every moment. As long as we remain externally oriented and not in the present moment, we can blame others and stay victims of their existence.

Here is one exercise that can help us to rediscover our childhoods and rewrite the present experiences of older painful events in a situation of safety and personal empowerment. By assuming the responsibility for our past, we can remember it with acceptance, clarity, and safety. This technique involves recreating the traumatic event or events in our lives with as much detail as possible. Therefore, it is advisable to have another person present to ensure our safety and to support us.

Visualizing and creating all the sensations of that event is sometimes easiest to do with your eyes closed. Sit or lie down in a comfortable position.

You may want some soft, soothing music in the background. This exercise is most effective when you become emotionally involved in your memories and thoughts. Have some facial tissue nearby in case you begin to cry. Don't hold back if you want to cry. However, always remember you are in control of your thoughts and you are no longer a victim of your past.

As you remember the faces, sounds, smells, and feelings you had, you may feel the exact same vulnerability, shame, guilt, or anger as the original event. Experiencing the event as close to reality as you remember is desirable because it is from this point that you can begin to take control of the situation. This means that you can now talk to and with the people who are present in your imaginary story. Because it is your story, you can even have the characters respond to you in a desired manner; they can now treat you with respect and dignity. While you are reliving this situation the way you choose, which is closest to your essence, it is also important that you allow the present-day you to enter your story. This means there are two of you present in the story, the younger you and the present-day you. The present-day you will take full responsibility for ensuring your safety and will protect the younger you from any of the other characters in your story. As your story unfolds and is created the way you want it to be, you will talk with the present you and tell that older you how much you appreciate the love and support. The present you will tell the younger you how precious and special you are.

From this point, imagine that the younger you enters the body of the present you so that you become one person with two lives, the present and younger you. Now travel forward in time to the next traumatic event in your life. As you recall the next event, know that the present you is always there to protect you and nurture you through these events. Remember the event as best you can. Assume a position of empowerment: you can ask questions of the characters, you can challenge them, you can respond with dignity, you can respond without fear, you can nurture yourself and other characters.

Continue this process until the you are back in the present moment. As you arrive in the present moment, the younger you is now a mature adult capable of taking care of your feelings and physical needs; the two of you are the best of friends. You can trust that both of you will always be there to take care of you and provide for you. Take a deep breath and exhale. Open your eyes slowly and pay attention to how you feel. You may feel light and airy, and the world may seem different. Life will seem easier but awkward because you are not accustomed to dealing with the present moment without the old attachments to your painful memories. It will feel like a weight has been lifted from your shoulders, while at the same time it may feel like you are walking in a new pair of shoes; you will be excited but a little uncomfortable. Also it is natural to wonder if this feeling will last. Don't be afraid; it will last as long as you stay in the present moment and focused on your essence. The moment you start to operate from fear you will lose the essence of what you want.

The time to experience what you want is now, and the two of you are ready and willing to give you what you want. After all, you deserve it; it is your essence!

Managing Our Expectations

The wildflower, before it blossoms,
looks like a weed.

In the world of the ego we require definitions, buckets, categories, and measurements to validate who we are. How we describe ourselves is precisely what keeps us locked in a world of limitations. Describing ourselves by job title, race, religion, nationality, school affiliation, and political party serves to validate our ego but does not bring us closer to the essence of what we truly want. Our ego ascribes certain expectations of how our lives should be when we deny our individuality and become part of a group. When our expectations are not met, we become disappointed and feel we are not acceptable. We use our own beliefs to tell us we failed. Even worse, we accept other people's judgments of us as accurate.

We are more than a physical description (fat, thin, black, white, brown, tall, short, etc.) or a job title (doctor, plumber, engineer, assembler, lawyer, teacher, clerk, etc.). All people have a purpose that is defined by their essence. When we live with purpose from our inner sense, life mysteriously provides for our sustenance and comfort. We do not have to struggle to make a living any longer. Our lives radiate harmony, and the world responds with generosity. Our expectations are replaced with trustworthy knowledge from our inner sense. This knowledge discloses a new realm of possibilities that we never knew existed. We can live without expectations and without effort if we allow our essence to guide us to the place we want to be.

Goal Setting

The cat which climbs the tree
to catch the bird forgets it cannot fly.

In western society our egos have left us with a mission to conquer and control things. A common practice is that of "goal setting." We use goal achievement as a statement of our worth; we like to say to ourselves and others, "Look what I've done." The purpose of a goal is to bring us fulfillment, a sense of accomplishment, and to boost our self-esteem. Contrary to logic, goals have precisely the opposite effect. In other words, our society encourages obsessive-compulsive behavior in the name of achieving a goal. Once we attain a goal we receive an immediate reward of gratification with a short-term "high" (the ego boost). However, once we reach a goal, it lacks value because it is only measurable in the context of the past. Without a new goal to replace the old one, there is no sense of purpose, so we continuously look for new goals to achieve. Goal setting can become an addiction by providing a convenient distraction from the emotional issues we wish to ignore regularly.

The goals we set in life often satisfy our ego but lack a common theme of purpose. Often we confuse our goals with our essence. Without essence, our accomplishments reward us with emotional and spiritual emptiness.

Goal-oriented people believe that life fulfillment comes from "doing." When we don't achieve a goal, we are classified and self-judged as inadequate, incompetent, and not capable. In our minds we become a failure, which makes us unacceptable. When we believe we are unacceptable, we experience low self-esteem. Our self-esteem determines if we are worthy of loving ourselves and accepting love from others. There is little value in playing this game. We cannot win because the game never ends; there is always someone else to impress. The alternative is to determine the essence of our being. If we stay focused on our essence, we increase our chances of experiencing what we really want in life. We never fail and we find a lasting reward that comes from the journey, and not from the destination!

Part Four

Steps to Heaven

❖   ❖   ❖

Chapter 11

≡ Home Free!

*The gateway to heaven is found in the stillness
of a beating heart and a quiet mind.*

The possibility exists for everyone to lead a more fulfilled life. Some of us recognize the opportunity to
improve our lives, while others continue to seek fulfillment
through their ego. If we make it through childhood, we can
consider ourselves fortunate. We owe gratitude to our primary caretakers. Our parents provide us the chance to
exercise our freedom of choice as adults. Despite the emotional pain, the bitterness, the abuse, or unfair treatment we
received from our families, we have the option to create a
new life. As adults, we can take full responsibility for our
lives. We can become reborn to our inner sense. This chapter identifies some additional steps that can help us begin

new lives of love, trust, and fulfillment. We will begin contributing to the healing of the human spirit. We will live in
harmony with the universe and all its energy. We will experience heaven in this life!

Personal History

History is what you learn from it.

Our personal history is the first step toward understanding the person we are today. Our experiences brought
us to this point in our lives, and at every moment of our
lives we face another decision point. As each moment slips
into the past, we set the direction of our future experiences;
we create our own life. Most of us experience life unaware
of how our fears, which stem from our thoughts of the past,
influence the decisions we make.

If we still are not sure of the impact our past is having on
our lives, we can start by examining our family relationships. We can uncover clues by asking ourselves how we
feel when we think of or talk to our families. How long have
we been playing the same roles with each person in our families? We can determine if our family experiences are affect-
ing our decision process by asking the following questions:

Do we resist new ideas?

Do we resist change?

Are we judgmental of others?

Do we need to be in control of our
physical environment?

Do we perceive the world as a dirty
and dangerous place?

Are we concerned that we will not be in a healthy, loving relationship?

Are we afraid that if we express ourselves on the job that we will be fired?

Are we still feeling resentment or anger toward a family member (friend, co-worker, boss)?

Are we dissatisfied with the way we look?

Are we afraid others are taking advantage of us?

Are we afraid of being too successful or of failing?

Are we afraid of not having sex?

Is the world competing with us?

If we answer "yes" to any of these questions, then we are still living from our past. We are still heavily influenced by our families and other experiences. Our lives are driven by the perception that history will repeat itself. History *will* repeat itself as long as we continue to base our decisions on the past. The only way to have a more fulfilled future is to welcome every moment of our lives as a unique and new experience. Of course, this requires that we trust our abilities to create something better than what we are currently experiencing.

Confession

Your decisions and actions are influenced by the summation of your past experiences.

We must acknowledge the impact our past is having on our lives. If we are not experiencing our essence, then our thought processes are keeping us discontented. Changing the way we think is a big step for most of us because we must be willing to admit we are perfect — we are equipped to live life with love, joy, and without effort — but still have feelings of being egotistical, afraid, lonely, and unhappy. While we confess to others we are not perfect, we often have a difficult time accepting ourselves. We either get consumed in our quest for perfection or we don't try because we are afraid the truth will prove our inadequacies. We seldom consider changing our definition of perfection. More importantly, we do not take responsibility for improving our lives emotionally. Fear of change, and not change itself, causes us to stay stuck in uncomfortable situations. In our attempt to avoid confronting fear, we experience the very thing we are afraid of, and we don't even realize it. For example, people who are afraid of loneliness will avoid an intimate relationship because they anticipate the termination of the relationship. So they avoid participating in intimate relationships and are lonely. In other words, their fear keeps them experiencing exactly what they don't want (a self-fulfilling prophecy).

If we allow fear to control our lives, we will never experience the power of our inner sense. We will give away our power to someone else. We will be disappointed frequently because we are not willing to confront our fears. A fulfilled life requires we take a leap of faith to get past our fears. When we jump into the world of the unknown, we realize the world of fear is just an illusion. Once we confront our fears, the lonely person will find love, the sick will find health, the fearful will find courage, the weak will find strength, and the angry will find peace.

Forgiveness

*Judge others not by the limits
of your own mind.*

In order for us to come closer to Heaven, we must be willing to forgive others and ourselves. Each person's pattern of behavior comes from emotional hurt and the need to feel acceptance. If we feel we have been a victim as an adult, it is partly because we are out of harmony with our essence and partly because the offender is acting out his or her hurt. Everyone acts out emotional hurt differently. Most of us abuse ourselves, and sometimes we are abusive to others. The degree of abuse depends on the severity of our emotional wounds. We can learn to let go of grudges and to release self-guilt.

Let's start forgiving those who have violated us, including ourselves. We can learn to accept our painful experiences and refrain from living in disharmony with our inner sense. With every moment that passes, we can pursue life with a new reality or we can continue to experience the mediocrity of our present lives. Forgiveness requires letting go of our attachment to the past; it requires the understanding, compassion, and trust that we can create a life consistent with our essence. We cannot let go of our past without letting go of our ego. Courage protects us from reliving the same experience in the same way again. We have nothing to fear if we truly know love.

Self-Acceptance

The bird that spreads its wings can fly.

After we learn forgiveness, we will be in a better position to accept the person we are and believe in the person we want to be. Accepting ourselves and knowing that we can create whatever we want is paramount to realizing our essence. When we learn to love ourselves and to trust ourselves, we enter a state of self-acceptance. We stop being critical and judgmental of ourselves. Although we may not have realized it yet, we are already perfect, otherwise we would not be here. We do not have to strive for perfection because we are already perfect. We are perfectly equipped to provide for ourselves without clinging to another person, a job, or any material possessions.

An important element of self-acceptance is to recognize that we are a part of nature. We are an integral part of the universe and its energy. When we accept ourselves, we will live in harmony with nature and allow our inner sense to balance our ego. Life is about harmony and balance. When we trust that our actions are a reflection of our inner sense, we won't need to worry about the consequences of what we do anymore. Our thoughts and actions will be in harmony with nature. We will no longer need to feel guilty. We can take full responsibility for our thoughts and actions.

No one can get to heaven without learning to accept themselves as they are. We can stop apologizing to others about the way we look, feel, and behave. We do not have to change what we do; we only have to define and to stay true to our essence. Change is a form of measurement. It measures our past against the present, and our perception of the future. An important lesson to learn about happiness is that we need to live in the moment. We will not fully experience the moment if we are too busy comparing it to the past or anticipating the future. Trusting our inner sense will ensure that we live according to our essence and in our personal Heaven, where we witness the miracle of the God within us.

Self-Respect

*How would you treat yourself differently
if you were in love with yourself?*

Once we learn to accept the persons we are, we also learn that we are the most important priority in our lives. Do not interpret this to mean that we have become selfish. To the contrary, the more we accept and respect ourselves, the more we learn the meaning of love. We can share our love with others. When we become the priority in our lives, we have the strength and integrity to share more with others. We assume full responsibility for our personal state of physical and mental health. We become our primary caretaker, and there is nothing more important than loving ourselves enough to honor our essence. When we nurture ourselves, we are in harmony with universal energy. If we have allowed parents, children, relatives, friends, jobs, possessions, religious habits, social obligations to become more important than ourselves, we are diminishing our abilities to be a truly loving person. When we demonstrate self-respect, we put our external affairs aside so that we can focus on our essence. Our ego feels satisfied when we focus on external affairs; however, we maintain our health when we live from our inner sense and not from our ego.

Humility

Humble waves return to the sea in silence.

Many of us are victims of our emotions. Ego keeps our emotions in an unnecessary state of conflict with our environment. For example, our pride may cause us to fight when we may not need to; when we are not treated with respect our pride usually intercedes. When our feelings are violated, we retaliate with anger and shame; we enter conflict with ourselves and others.

Pride is not worth fighting for; however, essence is — because it is the basis of our existence. Our self-worth is not determined by how others treat us, how much money we have, who loves us, or our position in society. No one else can devalue the worthiness of our being; only we can decide how valuable we are. In fact, we feel the greatest sense of respect when we pursue even socially demeaning activities with dignity. If we feel we are in a demeaning situation, our best solution is to stay focused on our essence. If we don't believe an activity is consistent with our essence, we can still exercise our choice not to undertake that activity. True pride is when we follow our essence and not our ego. This is known as integrity. When we are living within the integrity of our essence, what we do, or how others perceive us, will not matter; our inner sense will promote our best interest. The gate to Heaven will not open for those with little integrity.

Patience

Have the patience to sit and watch the transformation.

Life is dynamic because it is constantly transforming with the vibration of energy. Therefore, life is not measurable; there are no results. Unfortunately, most people have not yet realized that our expectations trap us in a state of anticipation. We are results-oriented and we devise ways to measure our progress. For example, time is a derivative of our human ingenuity, which serves to fulfill the needs of the ego. That means time, as we know it, is merely a measurement related to human perception. In the realm of pure energy, time is of no significance. Nature has its own timetable and we have used our observation of nature to define time (years, seasons, months, days, hours, minutes, seconds). In other words, things happen when they *do* — not when they *should*. This is important because socialization and education teaches us that life "should" be a certain way. These imposed expectations from childhood severely limit the mind to recognize possibilities that extend beyond our education. We become slaves to the clock. It controls our lives, defines when we sleep, eat, work, and play. Ironically, we have not devised a technique of measuring the energy transformation process in the universe. We can't accurately predict death or weather because we can't duplicate the dynamics of the universe or simulate exact conditions and circumstances in our laboratories or computer programs. Yet we continue to use our limited understanding of nature's dynamics to program our lives based on an artificial measurement called time. Unfortunately, most of us can only comprehend time in relation to our own life spans.

The illustration below gives the impression that energy transformation is progressive. This picture may help the human ego to understand the idea of energy transformation. However, transformation of energy is not progressive or regressive — it merely replicates itself in many forms. The issue of time is not relevant to the diagram below because time is not what determines our transformation; our inner sense does. That explains why we don't all die at the same age.

| Energy | Human Passage | Transformation |

*Time stands still except in the
measurement of its movement.*

We believe our lives should evolve at a rate defined for
us by society. We see life as cause-and-effect relationships.
Therefore, we expect our actions to generate specific results.
Our expectations tell us we will see results within a given
time frame. If the results don't appear when we expect
them to, we pass judgment in terms of success or failure. In
fact, most of us are so afraid that we won't get what we
want that we have almost no patience to wait during the
gestation period of our dreams. Instead, we often act prematurely or make fear-based decisions. When we start to
live in relation to our inner sense, the cause-and-effect
model ceases to apply. Our expectations fade into oblivion
as we enter the world of true intelligence and knowing.
Without the boundaries of time, we become involved with
life and life becomes involved with us.

It often takes years in the human development process
to deprogram our ego and to trust our inner sense.
However, we don't have to endure our pain any longer
than we decide to. If we can forget our need to see results
and learn to live within our present moment, we will find
that our essence is at the fingertips of our next thought and
our next emotion. So, what is next? There is no next. Next
will never come except in the present moment. If we concern ourselves with the future, it will never come. Now is
the only moment that ever exists and how we emotionally
experience each moment is our choice.

*We endure the lessons of our ego in order
to graduate to a more fulfilled existence.*

The Final Decision

Share the best that you are,
that this earth may heal
in your being.

Problems, like time, are the creations of our ego. There is
no instant approach to resolving problems. Problems exist
because we create them mentally in our search for happiness. We believe happiness is an end result, and when we
are not happy, we conclude we have problems. Problems,
like happiness, are always in a state of transformation.
Therefore, we experience happiness when we participate in
and witness the transformation process called life.

We live a good portion of our lives like mushrooms, in
the dark and covered with manure, waiting for someone to
come and pick us and take us to the light. Once we discover
our essence, we have the opportunity to harvest ourselves.
We don't have to wait to be chosen by some higher being.
That higher being is us. We are empowered to create our personal Heaven. Living true to our essence is what determines
if we enter the Kingdom of Heaven. Our experience in life is
nothing more than the transformation of energy. Our
thoughts and feelings are merely energy which transforms
our reality. The decisions we derive from our thoughts are
what determine our actions and emotions. We can choose
between the misery and suffering of the ego (past and future)
or the peace and tranquility of our inner sense (present
moment). Once we are aware of our fears, shame, and ego,
we can begin our transformation. The decision to risk losing
our ego is the toughest step to take. However, we can discover Heaven by focusing on our essence and taking a leap
of faith that we can live without ego. Our essence and our
inner sense are the two halves of the treasure map that can

guide us to the divine state of Heaven. We are all Angels waiting to fulfill our purpose in life. Living life according to our essence is our purpose. It is the essence of living!

A marvelous thing happens
on the way to our graves —
Life!

AFTERWARDS

The key unlocks the closed door that separates the shared space on either side.

After reading this book you may be compelled to incorporate some of the ideas presented into your life. It occurred to me that to truly implement the concepts or methods proposed would require that you be internally oriented. The only way this is possible is to not be attached to the book or its author but to embrace the essence of its content. This means that to truly live the life you want, you will need to be aware of your power and inherent knowledge. To refer back to the book for guidance is, in fact, a demonstration of being externally oriented and does not acknowledge your trust and inner sense. It is my desire that you not be dependent on this book to live your essence but that you trust your inner sense to choose, in each moment, only those thoughts that will allow you to experience the essence of what you want at that time. All other answers will be revealed to you after you live that moment. For this reason, I would like to ask you to forward this book to a friend or stranger once you have captured its essence. I look forward to meeting you in joy, peace, and love on your journey through the universe and in this Heaven I call earth.

Every page was a tree once
Every word was a thought once
Every story was an experience once
Every life was passion once
Every soul was a spirit once
Every illusion was reality.

❖   ❖   ❖

ABOUT THE AUTHOR

David B. Bolen, II, analyzed his exploration into the realm of total being and summarized this ten-year experience in *The* ESSENCE *of* LIVING. He grew up on three continents and has traveled extensively since his youth. Prior to committing to his purpose in life, he worked for sixteen years in several large corporations as a marketing strategist, planner, and consultant. While he was the director of international business development, he shared his philosophy with people worldwide and found that at the essence of our being we each aspire to a common human experience. He credits his personal discoveries to his family, friends, and a universal perspective on living. He has a bachelors' degree from the University of Colorado, and he proclaims a standing of L.C.H.B. (Licensed and Certified Human Being). He and his wife are co-founders of Shared Knowledge, a company committed to aiding those who seek personal awareness and empowerment.

ORDER FORM

Please send me: <u>Quantity</u> x <u>Price</u> = <u>Total Amount</u>

The ESSENCE *of* LIVING:
Reaching Beyond Global Insanity.
    ISBN: 0-9641909-0-7   _____ $11.95 $_____

(Discounts available for quantities. Please contact us!)

Shipping and handling fee (per book):
Standard fourth class mail in the U.S.A. _____ $2.00 $_____
Standard first class mail in the U.S.A.   _____ $3.25 $_____

    TOTAL *(includes book(s) plus shipping and handling)* $_____
    All payments are due in U.S. dollar currency only.

Enclosed is this order form and my payment in full:
    Check one: ____Money Order ____Check
    Make checks payable to: New Verity Publishing

——————————————————— fold here for mailing ———————————

Please charge this purchase to my credit card/*Circle one:*

    VISA/Mastercard — Account Number: _____
    Expiration Date: Mo._____Day_____Year_____
    Daytime telephone number: Area code (___)_____
    (In case we have a question about your order.)

Card Holder's Signature:_____

Please mail my copies of *The* ESSENCE *of* LIVING to the address below:

    Your name:_____
    Company:_____
    Street Address:_____
    City:_____State_____Zip_____
    Country:_____

Thank You for Your Order!

- -

We would like to thank you for selecting The ESSENCE *of* LIVING: *Reaching Beyond Global Insanity by David B. Bolen, II. If you would like additional copies of this book, you may order them directly by sending us the completed form above, or contact your local bookseller.*

New Verity Publishing
726 Keene Dr., Medford, OR 97504
Order toll free: (800) 683-7489 • Fax: (503) 857-0274

do not staple — tape here

New Verity Publishing
thanks you for your order!

❖

───────────── fold here ─────────────

NEW VERITY

PUBLISHING

place
stamp
here

TO:

NEW VERITY PUBLISHING
726 KEENE DRIVE
MEDFORD, OR 97504

tear here

tear here